# Mahārāsa Mañjūṣā

The Bhaktivedanta Research Center is an academic center of excellence dedicated to preserve, research and teach the philosophies and cultural heritage of India.

## Vaishnava Studies Series

The *Vaishnava Studies Series* in association with the Bhaktivedanta Research Center offers a platform for the latest research in Vaishnavism in India and globally. This series welcomes historical, philosophical and ethical studies in various Vaishnava traditions with emphasis on important texts including annotated translations of primary sources. It also publishes new research work that explores the ways in which Vaishnavism contributes to social and cultural change or adaptation and how it lends meaning to individual and collective lives.

# Mahārāsa Mañjūṣā:

## Sacred Poetry of the Divine Dance

Nandadāsa


Translation and Commentary by

Prakriti Goswami

Foreword by

David L. Haberman, Ph.D.



MANDALA

San Rafael Los Angeles London

For my brother – in his departure,
he unfolded the divine play of Śrī Hari for me.

आत्मा यावत्प्रपन्नोऽभूत्तावद्वै रमते हरिः।
सोऽन्तःकरणसम्बन्धी तिरोधत्ते हरिश्च सः॥

As long as the self remains in his refuge, Hari delights with it.
He is the kin of the mind, who conceals himself when the mind wavers.
*Subodhinī: 10/23/9*

# Contents

Acknowledgments ix
Foreword xi
A Note on Translation and Transliteration xv

## Part I: The Introductory Framework of Nandadāsa's Work

1. The Historical Context and Religious Structure of the Poetry 3
   1.1 *Puṣṭimārga* – The *Bhāgavata-Bhakti* Tradition of Vallabha 4
   1.2 Theo-aesthetics of *Bhāgavata* and its Vedāntic Underpinning 11
   1.3 *Rāsapañcādhyāyī* – The Dance of the Self with the Supreme 13

2. *Aṣṭa-Chāpa* – Their Origin and the Legacy 21
   2.1 The Emergence of Devotional Music in India 22
   2.2 The Era of *Dhrupad* and the Rise of Regional Saint-poets 24
   2.3 The Structure of *Havelī Saṅgīta* 27
   2.4 Liturgical and Exegetical use of *Havelī Saṅgīta* 31

3. Nandadāsa: As a Devotee and a Poet 35

## Part II: Nandadāsa's Poetic Rendition of the *Rāsapañcādhyāyī*

1. *Śuka-Stuti*: Paean to the Orator of the *Bhāgavata* (1-21) 45
2. *Vṛndāvana-Varṇana*: Describing the Stage of the Divine Dance (22-54) 53
3. Chapter I: The Beginning of *Rāsalīlā* and the Call of the Flute (55-133) 65
4. Chapter II: Pangs of Separation (134-180) 93
5. Chapter III: The Song of the *Gopikās* (181-195) 111
6. Chapter IV: Kṛṣṇa's Solace to the *Gopikās* (196-222) 117
7. Chapter V: *Mahārāsa* – Culmination of the Ecstatic Dance (223-286) 127
8. *Phala-Śruti*: Significance of *Mahārāsa* (287-301) 151

Selected Bibliography 157
Index 161

# Acknowledgments

IT IS IMPOSSIBLE to appreciate everyone involved in the shaping of this book. However, I offer special thanks to my teachers, colleagues, and friends who supported me throughout my journey. I express my gratitude towards Dr. David Haberman, my advisor at Indiana University, who walked me through the nuances of translation and held my hand at every step. It is impossible to imagine writing my first book without his supervision, and I owe the successful completion of this book to his continuous support. I attribute all the errors to my inexperience, hoping I will continue to learn as I progress through my journey. I will also appreciate my supportive colleague and friend, Jessica Merritt, who read some of my translations' first drafts, walked me through Dr. Haberman's comments, and helped me trust my writings whenever I felt blocked by my thoughts.

I owe immense gratitude towards the Bhaktivedanta Research Centre, especially Dr. Sumanta Rudra; this project would not have been conceived without his initiative and unrelenting fostering. I am also grateful to Mandala Publishing for trusting the scribblings of an unversed author and turning it into a competent venture. I hold special gratitude for my granduncle and *śikśā*-guru, Shri Shyammanohar Goswami. Though his blessings have touched many who attempt to understand the cryptic world of Śrī Vallabhācārya's words, I feel incredibly graced by his guiding presence in my life.

I want to expressly thank my parents and their unconditional assistance; their love and blessings build my path. My father named this book to reflect the treasure trove of *mahārāsa*, as he has been a treasure trove of knowledge for me. While he was the first go-to source for every inquiry I had, I am specifically grateful for his continuous research on the musicology of Puṣṭimārga, a topic with extremely limited resources. And above all, I thank my mother for her uninhibited patience and support that made the most formidable steps of my journey seem effortless.

Seeing that I wrote this book while going through a challenging period of my life, I ultimately believe that it is the unbounded blessings of Śrī Kṛṣṇa and the words of Nandadāsa, his most excellent devotee, that kept me going. I would not think of translating the powerful words of such wonderful devotional poetry without the grace of my lord, Madanmohana, the one with a crooked leg, crooked smile, and crooked ways! I am ultimately beholden to him.

# Foreword

ALTHOUGH ONE FREQUENTLY hears these days that money makes the world go round, I am old school enough to still hold that it is passion that does so. Early Vedāntic scriptures concur, identifying passion as the very force behind all creative expression—including the creation of the world itself. Understanding how to recognize and participate in this passionate process has been the goal of numerous religious traditions. The great Kṛṣṇaite devotional traditions of Braja are assuredly among them. Instead of extinguishing desire as many ascetic traditions recommend, they have devised ways to use human desire to connect with God in a loving relationship. The great sixteenth-century *aṣṭa-chāpa* poet Nandadāsa is one of my favorites among the early talented poets of Braja; he was a very passionate man who composed exquisite poetry. His life story tells us that he was even a bit of a shameful *badmāś*, a "bad boy," whose undisciplined passion led him to fall madly in love with the wife of another man, scandalously vowing not to eat each day until he had seen her face. His lustful ways were eventually transformed into a divine love through an inadvertent encounter with the Yamuna River, the embodied form of the great Goddess whose distinctive role is to initiate souls into the divine love affair with Kṛṣṇa. In one of his poems Nandadāsa exclaims: "Śrī Yamunā showers amazing grace upon her devotees." After this transformative encounter Nandadāsa dedicated his life to worshipping and writing poetry about his beloved Śrī Kṛṣṇa.

While Nandadāsa's impassioned nature led him to an improper love for another man's wife, it also formed a solid basis for his passionate attachment to God. It is no wonder then, that he was drawn to the

Rāsapañcādhyāyī, the five chapters in the *Bhāgavata Purāṇa* that narrate the passionate love dance (*rāsa-līlā*) that is the pinnacle of the loving connection with God for the Kṛṣṇaite traditions that follow the *Bhāgavata*. On a beautiful autumn evening Kṛṣṇa calls his lovers to a lush forest with his flute and commences the divine love dance with them. This dance is personal for his lovers, as Kṛṣṇa is able to transform himself into a great variety of forms for an intimate engagement with each of them individually. Many, however, don't come to this episode by way of a direct reading the *Bhāgavata Purāṇa*. Rather, it is often encountered through song, dance, poetry, drama, and other forms of artistic expression. Nandadas's poem is a superb illustration of this; this is a poem meant to be visualized. Really more than visualized—for the connoisseurs of this poetic tradition it offers a doorway into joyful participation in the very scene that the poem depicts. Prakriti Goswami has done a great service to English readers by making available to them her excellent and vivid translation of the *Mahārāsa Mañjūṣā*, Nandadāsa's own unique glimpse of the sacred *rāsa* dance that has been celebrated for centuries.

For many reasons the fairly esoteric philosophy and practices of the Puṣṭimārga Vaiṣṇava tradition founded by Vallabhāchaya have been scarcely studied and little understood by the English-speaking world. Prakriti Goswami's introduction to her translation of Nandadāsa's spectacular poem provides an edifying corrective to much of this. Perhaps most productive, although she does not use the Sanskrit terms, she introduces readers to Vallabhāchaya's fascinating concept of *viruddha-dharma-āśyaya*, the coexistence of seemingly contradictory or paradoxical characteristics. This applies in subtle ways to both the nature of God as well as the perspective and worshipful practices of the devotee. Kṛṣṇa in the Puṣṭimārga is understood to be the ultimate formless non-dual (*adviata*) reality of Brahman, and simultaneously, a unique beloved form that allows relational connectivity in the intimacy nurtured in the devotee's everyday practice of loving worship (*sevā*). Nandadāsa tells us in the *Mahārāsa Mañjūṣā* that Kṛṣṇa is the all-pervasive ultimate reality: "The Supreme Lord, is here, always very near, residing as the inner controller, of every aspect of the sphere" (293). And yet for his cowherdess lovers he appears as an attractive form: "His beautiful black body, is adorned with a yellow robe. As if passion personified and arose, wearing a garment of love" (114). Moreover, Kṛṣṇa takes on seemingly contradictory forms such as a mischievous child or a romantic lover to meet a devotee's particular disposition in the intimacy of say a mood of parental affection or an amorous one, as is the case in this poem. The devotee engages a form Kṛṣṇa with an individual passionate love that is accompanied by an awareness of the vast and supreme identity of Kṛṣṇa as the totality of all reality.

We see here the enigmatic bringing together of unbounded universality with individual particularity. The devotional poetry of Braja tracks a similar move. The general story of the divine love dance involving Kṛṣṇa and his lovers is available in the Rāsapañcādhyāyī section of the *Bhāgavata Purāṇa*, but the tradition regards the particular story told by Nandadāsa in his poem *Mahārāsa Mañjūṣā* as the result of the direct vision he had of this dance himself. Thus, we find in this enchanting poem details and incidents not available in the usual scripture. Through poetic vision the playful divine love dance thus swells increasingly in an ever-expanding circle. With her deep knowledge of the poetic traditions of Braja, as well as the philosophy and religious practices of the Puṣṭimārga, Prakriti Goswami has produced a wonderful translation of this intricate poem which provides a rich opportunity for readers to swing into its delightful and dramatic action.

David L. Haberman, Ph.D.
Professor Emeritus, Religious Studies
Indiana University

# A Note on Translation and Transliteration

IN THE INTRODUCTORY passages, I have followed the general guidelines of transliterating Sanskrit words, except for some popular names that I have not Sanskritized. For instance, a Sanskritized transliteration of Tansen would be Tānasena, but I transliterated it as "Tānsen" by following the standardised spelling with a minor insertion of a length mark (-) to guide the pronunciation.

While transliterating Nandadāsa's poem, I have followed the conventions of Braja Bhāṣa speech sounds such as using *bandana* instead of *vandana*. Particularly, I have retained the final a's which usually go unpronounced in Hindi but is a significant pronunciation in both conversational Braja Bhāṣa as well as in the poetic meters of its composition. Hence, I go with "Braja" instead of "Braj." Nasalisation of the vowels forms the key to most of the speech sounds in Braja Bhāṣa. While some of these nasalisations only have phonetic significance, there are also a few cases in which this process changes the meaning of the word entirely. For instance, the word *kahā* means "what;" however, when the vowel "a" is nasalised in *kahā̃*, the meaning changes to "where." To denote this specific nasalisation, I have employed the diacritic mark (~) on the top of the vowel to mark its nasalisation and distinguish it from the variations in consonant and vowel sounds of "n." Thus, I have used *kũvara* instead of *kuṁvara* to denote the nasalisation of the vowel "u." On the other hand, in the word *kuṅkuma*, it is not the vowel "u" that is nasalised; rather it is the guttural nasal "ङ," which is conventionally denoted with the diacritical mark "ṅ." Similarly, in words like *raṅga* pronounced like *ing* as in "sing" and *pañca* pronounced with palatized *ni* as in "onion." In words like these, the diacritics denote nasal consonants of the guttural, palatals, and the retroflex groups. "Retroflex" consonants marked with a dot under the consonant such as (*ṭ*, *ḍ*, *ṇ*) are pronounced by touching the tongue to the roof of the mouth to produce "retroflex" sound and both *ś* and *ṣ* are pronounced like *sh* as in "ship." Dental consonants (l, n, d) are pronounced like French l, d, n and aspirated consonants are pronounced directly such as *bh* in clubhouse or *th* in boathouse.

Finally, the poem is composed in *rolā* metre, which is a sub-category of *mātrika chanda* in which every line is divided into 24 instants (*mātrā*) and 11th and 13th instants have a poetic long pause. It is the common metre for poetic compositions, and thus is also known by the name *kāvya-chanda* or "poetic metre." The lines rhyme in pairs, forming an *aa-bb-cc* rhyming pattern and each pair form a single verse. My translation progresses verse by verse and the order of the lines is strictly followed, which means that the first part of the translation only expresses the first line of the verse while the second part of the translation, separated by a single line space, expresses the second line of the verse. I have tried to keep the poetics of the original composition alive as much as possible, but the primary focus is on producing literal, word for word translation as far as possible. Some specific adjectives, metaphors, and words associated with both the poetics and culture of Braja are glossed in footnotes to facilitate the reading.

PART I

# The Introductory Framework of Nandadāsa's Work

ONE

# The Historical Context and Religious Structure of the Poetry

THE *RĀSA-LĪLA* IS celebrated as one of the most important activities of Kṛṣṇa, as it is understood to be a dance of divine love wherein Kṛṣṇa multiplies himself to partner with each of the participants in an ecstatic union of loving joy. The revered episode that is expressed in five chapters of the *Bhāgavata Purāṇa*, known as the *Rāsapañcādhyāyī*, literally "five-chapters-of-the-rāsa," was rendered into beautiful poetic form by the sixteenth-century poet Nandadāsa. Nandadāsa was one of the eight principal devotional poets (*aṣṭa-chāpa*) of the Vallabha tradition, which is also known as the Path of Grace (*Puṣṭimārga*). Of these *aṣṭa-chāpa* poets, while Sūrdās and Paramānandadāsa are widely popular in the devotional folk literature of northern India, Nandadāsa's poetry is mostly known only within the community of *Puṣṭimārga* followers. Through the translation of one of Nandadāsa's most comprehensive poetries, this essay aims to sketch his work on the canvas of his devotional theology and fill in with the colours of regional poetics employed by him. While Nandadāsa follows the order of the unfolding of the divine dance as per the *Bhāgavata Purāṇa*'s description, he begins by setting up the stage of the narrative and concludes by highlighting the devotional significance of the episode.

Before I trace this scheme of narration, it is crucial to situate it in its historical context and outline the religious foundation upon which the poetic structure has been constructed. The following introductory sections are designed to take the reader from the outermost layer, which is the religious backdrop of the text, to the inner core, which is exploring the poet's frame of thought through the accounts of his life and devotional inclination. The final section of the introduction sketches the order of Nandadāsa's work and indicates the pattern of translation and annotation followed through the book.

## 1.1 *Puṣṭimārga* - The *Bhāgavata-Bhakti* Tradition of Vallabha

*Bhakti* as a form of religious expression has been primarily studied from the perspective of "the bhakti movement," especially since the beginning of the twentieth century. As noted by many scholars, this considerably recent term has projected the idea of historical continuity through the development of *bhakti*, often at the cost of neglecting the undeniable heterogeneity in the style, narrative, purpose, and theological backdrop that defines the distinctiveness of these movements across India.[1] Some of these regional forms and styles of *bhakti* are elaborated expressions of the idea of *bhakti* propounded by the Vedāntic preceptors, which were often exegetically based on the Purāṇic scriptures, especially the *Bhāgavata*.

However, before we describe the central position that the *Bhāgavata* occupies in Vallabha's tradition, it is crucial to highlight the Vedāntic foundations upon which Vallabha builds his philosophical structure, to understand what distinguishes his hermeneutical approach from other Vedānta schools. The development of the Vedāntic philosophy is often divided into historical timeframes, namely, the early Vedāntic schools that were formulated before the compilation of the *Brahmasūtras* and the later schools that were formulated after the *Brahmasūtras* were configured into its present format. The *Brahmasūtras*, which are an axiomatic summary of the Upaniṣadic philosophy, are traditionally attribute to Vyāsa, the arranger of the Vedic texts, whose identity has been a matter of extensive scholarly debate and hence, the authorship of the texts attributed to him are often loosely stated. Against the traditional views, *Brahmasūtras* are believed to be compiled by several authors over a span of hundreds of years, and its present form is speculated to have been configured around 400 to 450 BCE.[2] These divisions are of hermeneutical significance, for they define the epistemological structure of the Vedānta schools. While the early Vedānta schools are largely lost to us, the exponents of the later Vedānta

1 Patton E. Burchette, *Genealogy of Devotion: Bhakti, Tantra, Yoga and Sufism in North India* (New York: Columbia University Press, 2019), 1-26.

2 Andrew J. Nicholson, *Unifying Hinduism: Philosophy and Identity in Indian Intellectual History* (New York: Columbia University Press, 2013), 26.

schools begin their scriptural exegeses with their commentaries on the *Brahmasūtras*, and develop their worldview by quoting scriptural references from the verses of the Vedas and the *Upaniṣads*, the *Brahmasūtras*, the *Bhagavadgītā*, and at times, also the *Bhāgavata*. Of these ten later schools of Vedānta, as listed by R. Chaudhury in her work,[3] five are noted to be the prominent ones, which are known as the "*pañca-Vedānta-sampradāya*." These are the *Kevalādvaita* (Absolute Monism) of Śaṃkara, *Viśiṣṭādvaita* (Qualified Monism) of Rāmānuja, the *Svābhāvikadvaitādvaita* (Natural Dualism-Non-dualism) of Nimbārka, *Bhedavāda* (Doctrine of Difference) of Madhva, and the *Śuddhādvaita* (Pure Non-dualism) of Vallabha. Although these Vedāntic exponents adopt different hermeneutical structure to construct their exegetical positions, they uniformly agree on the incontestable authority of the Vedas and the *Upaniṣads*, the *Brahmasūtras*, and the *Bhagavadgītā*, which form a triad that is collectively known as the *prasthānatrayī* in the Vedānta tradition that developed after Śaṃkara. Vallabha contributes to this three-fold system of scriptural testimony by adding the *Bhāgavata* as an all-encompassing and culminative testimony of the scriptural inquiries, and thus designs a system commonly referred as *pramāṇa-catuṣṭaya* (four-fold means of knowledge).

Thus, taking a somewhat unconventional position in the trajectory of the Vedānta schools, the epistemological system of Vallabha hermeneutically views the *Bhāgavata* as a more detailed exposition of the ideas expressed in the *Brahmasūtras*, and not as a text that conflicts with the descriptions of *nirguṇa* Brahman in the Vedānta. In the beginning of his exegetical trilogy,[4] he systematically establishes the *Bhāgavata* as a comprehensive treatise that eradicates all the doubts relating to scriptures.[5] Thus, his hermeneutical exegeses situate the *Bhāgavata* as the culmination of scriptural inquiry, while his devotional path (*Puṣṭimārga)* is centred around the Kṛṣṇa devotional motifs of the *Bhāgavata*, which are

3 Roma Chaudhury, *Ten Schools of The Vedānta – Part 1* (Calcutta: Rabindra Bharti University, 1973), 19.

4 This trilogy, known as the *Tatvārtha-dīpa-nibandha*, forms one of the key works of Vallabha's Vedāntic exegeses. The first two parts of this work, namely, the *Śāstrārtha* (Meaning of Scriptures) and *Sarvanirṇaya* (Pronouncement on all Disputations), discuss Vallabha's critique on Vedic and non-Vedic theologies and philosophical systems. The third part is known as *Bhāgavatārtha*, which is a laconic commentary on the *Bhāgavata* and is often accompanied by a full-scale commentary entitled, *Subodhinī*.

5 *Śāstrartha* 7; *Tatvārtha-dīpa-nibandha*, edited by Shaym M. Goswami (Kolhapur: Śrīvallabhavidyāpīṭha-Śrīviṭṭhaleśaprabhucaraṇāśrma Trust, 1982), 1.

rooted in Vraja, a region located in the north of India. The devotional path of *Puṣṭimārga* is characterised by the practice of *puṣṭi-bhakti* (grace-filled devotion), and the key idea outlined is indeed the correlation between the divine grace and devotion in the spiritual journey of the aspirant. Hence, it is significant to understand the concept of both grace and devotion as defined by Vallabha to understand the development of *Puṣṭimārga*, which is the very framework of Nandadāsa's devotional poetry.

The *Śuddhādvaita* ideal of devotion is aphoristically defined in *Śāstrārtha* 42 as an unswerving love for God (*sneha*) classified by a mindful awareness of his glorious magnificence and essential form (*māhātmya*).[6] This definition encapsulates the paradoxical qualities of the supreme deity Kṛṣṇa, and the resultant dichotomy in the ritual praxis of the path. Kṛṣṇa, although lovingly described as the adorably mischievous child of Yaśodā (*yaśodotsaṅgalālitya*), is simultaneously the gloriously transcendental Lord who reigns supreme over the entire creation (Bhagavān) as well as the formless Absolute (Brahman) within whom subsists the perceivable and non-perceivable universe.[7] Vallabha defines the process of cultivating firm devotion as one that involves an interplay of devotional service (*sevā*) and development of an awareness about the supreme form of Kṛṣṇa (*kathā*), in a continuous and unbroken succession.[8] His concept of *sevā* is a highly personalised form of devotion to the Lord based on the idea and practice of *samarpaṇa*, which is a volitionally dedicated engagement of physical body (*tana*), emotional expression (*bhāva*), and material wealth (*vitta*), solely in the service of a personal embodied form of Kṛṣṇa-for-worship (*sevya-svarūpa*).[9] Such *sevya-svarūpas* are exclusively and distinctly sanctified for, and hence belong to, those devotees who after being initiated in the sect desire to worship him in their own homes (*gṛhe-sthitvā*) and without being distracted by worldly engagements (*avyāvṛttaḥ*).[10] The

6 Ibid, 80.

7 Ibid, 95-96.

8 *Puṣṭividhānam*, edited by Shyam M. Goswami (Gujarat: Śrī Vallabhācārya Trust, 2004), 377.

9 This refers to the consecration ceremony (*puruṣottama-pratiṣṭhā*) of Kṛṣṇa's image, performed by the gurus of the sect. This image is then referred as *sevya-svarūpa* or "Kṛṣṇa-for-worship," which is the translation taken from James D. Redington, *The Grace of Lord Krishna: The Sixteen Verse-Treatises (Ṣoḍaśagranthāḥ) of Vallabhacharya* (Delhi: Sri Satguru Publications, 2000), 68. An extensive account of this devotional practice can be found in Peter Bennett's *Krishna's Own Form: Image Worship in Puṣṭi Mārga* (1993).

10 This daily ritual of personalised image-worship is the common theme found across Vallabha's *Ṣoḍaśa-granthāḥ* and its commentaries, such as in *Siddhāntarahasyam* (Vol. 1; 21-23),

distinguishing feature of *sevā* is *bhāva*, which incorporates the subjective affectivities of the devotee while also vicariously embodying in oneself the prototypical parental love of Yaśodā (*vātsalya-bhāva*) for her child and the paradigmatic passionate love of the *gopikās* (*mādhurya-bhāva*) for their beloved. This involvement of parental love and passionate love would seem to be an engagement of contradictory emotions within one devotee. However, Vallabha proclaims that the one who cognises Kṛṣṇa as the abode of contrary attributes who is the subject and the object of all emotions is indeed the true devotee. Such a devotee worships the Lord of Vraja (Kṛṣṇa) always (*sarvadā*) and with all forms of emotions (*sarva-bhāvena*).[11] This requires a higher state of mental attuning which is developed through *kathā*, which is a recitation of the names and the narratives of the Lord. This process fosters a cognitive-spiritual awareness of Kṛṣṇa as both the supreme deity of the theistic liturgy (Bhagavān) and the formless absolute being who is one with the cosmos (Brahman). The cognition of Kṛṣṇa as Brahman leads to the knowledge of one's own self (*svarūpa-jñāna*) as a manifestation of Brahman.[12] The cognition of Kṛṣṇa as Bhagavān, then, is a reminder that duality is a playful expression of the divine bliss (*ānandasya harerlīlā*), which is to be joyfully accepted as the divine will.[13] Thus, while the former cognition makes one understand that one is a part of Brahman (*brahmāṃśa*), establishing absolute non-duality (*advaita*) between individual self and Supreme Self, the latter cognition makes one cultivate one's existence as a part of Bhagavān (*bhagavadaṃśa*), establishing a playful duality (*līlātmaka-dvaita*) between deity and devotee on the landscapes of devotional love. Vallabha thus outlines an ideal devotee as the one who directly experiences the absolute non-difference and yet feels blessed by submitting volitionally to the divine supreme will that manifests as the duality between the worshipper and the worshipped in and through worldly experiences.

---

*Siddhāntamuktāvalī* (Vol. 1; 20-21), *Bhaktivardhinī* (Vol. 2; 2-3), et al. The idea presented in this section is a summarised account of the devotional praxis developed in these treatises and their commentaries. The text referred to is a compilation of these sixteen treatises with their Sanskrit commentaries, which is distributed in three volumes. See *Ṣoḍaśagranthāḥ*, edited by Shyam M. Goswami (Bombay: Śrī Vallabhācārya Trust, 1980).

11 *Puṣṭividhānam*, edited by Shyam M. Goswami (Gujarat: Śrī Vallabhācārya Trust, 2004), 312.

12 *Tatvārtha-dīpa-nibandha*, edited by Shyam M. Goswami (Kolhapur: Śrīvallabhavidyāpīṭha-Śrīviṭṭhaleśaprabhucaraṇāśrma Trust, 1982), 68-70.

13 Vallabhācārya, *Bhāgavatārtha*, edited by Shyam M. Goswami (Kolhapur: Śrī Vallabha-vidyāpīṭha-Śrī Viṭṭhaleśaprabhucaraṇāśrma Trust, 1983), 87.

Vallabha formally defines *puṣṭi* at the *Bhāgavatārtha* 6.2 as "the form of Kṛṣṇa's grace that overcomes unfavourable period of time (*kāla*), an inexcusable action (*karma*), and an inappropriate nature (*svabhāva*)."[14] To grasp the primary meaning of the term "*puṣṭi*" on the path of grace, I highlight Puruṣottama's (1668-1725)[15] commentary on the *Puṣṭipravāhamaryādabheda*, which is one of Vallabha's sixteen treatises and discusses the difference between (the paths of) grace, flow, and limitations.[16] In the beginning of his commentary, Puruṣottama raises an interesting query – if all the *jīvas* evolve ontologically as the manifestation of Brahman's *sat* and *cit* aspects, then why is it that only a few are eligible to attain the supreme Lord (*puruṣottama-prāptī*). He answers by referring to a number of scriptural sources to support the three-fold hierarchization laid down by Vallabha, which places grace-filled selves (*puṣṭi-jīvas*) at the apex, and the rule-bound selves (*maryādā-jīvas*) and the worldly selves (*pravāhī-jīvas*) at the intermediate level and the lowest level respectively. Of these, the blessed individuals known as "*puṣṭi-jīvas*" are the ones who are chosen (*varaṇa*) by the supreme Lord based on their ability to engage in one-pointed (*ekāgraha*) and undiluted (*śuddha*) devotion. Further, the *puṣṭi-jīvas* and the *maryādā-jīvas* are categorised as *daivī* (godly) based on their inclination to strive for salvific objectives, while the *pravāhī-jīvas* are categorised as *āsurī* (demonic) based on their excessive indulgence in the worldly pleasures. Puruṣottama defines these worldly-selves as the ones who are flowing uninterruptedly in the cycle of births and deaths since the beginning of the creation (*sargaparamparayā-avicchedana*).[17] I argue that this hierarchization outlines a divine arrangement of the selves into these categories, which can only be altered by the supremely sovereign divine will. Hence, we can observe that liberation, which for Vallabha is a state of being in eternal service of Kṛṣṇa, is only attainable by the virtue of being

14 Vallabhācārya, *Bhāgavatārtha*, edited by Shyam M. Goswami (Jodhpur: Sri Subodhinī Prakāśana Maṇḍal, 1971), 199.

15 The traditional genealogies vary about his dates, such as 1657 or 1670, etc. See A.D. Shastri, *Puruṣottamajī: A Study* (Surat: Chunilal Gandhi Vidyabhava, 1966), 28.

16 Puruṣottama is widely regarded as one of the greatest commentators of Vallabha's sect, such that the presence of a commentary by him on a text is taken to authenticate the attribution of that text to Vallabha. For a detailed study of the *Puṣṭipravāhamaryāda* and its various commentaries, see F. Smith, "Predestination and Hierarchy," *Journal of Indian Philosophy* 39 (2011), 173-227.

17 *Ṣoḍaśagranthāḥ*, edited by Shyam M. Goswami (Bombay: Śrī Vallabhācārya Trust, 1980), 35.

"divinely chosen" and not through the individual efforts of the finite self.[18] Puruṣottama refers to the frequently quoted *Kaṭha Upaniṣad* verse[19] to support this argument, and asserts that the embracement of the devotional path is itself completely dependent on the divine grace.[20] The term "path of grace" thus outlines this unconditional suzerainty of divine grace over an individual's soteriological endeavours. However, this "power-dynamic" set forth by the concept of *puṣṭi* is radically revised by Vallabha when he illustrates the highest order of *bhakti* as that in which the Lord himself becomes "dependent" on the supreme devotees, rather than the other way around.

For instance, at the *Bhāgavata* 9.4.66, Kṛṣṇa proclaims, "they (*gopikās*) have controlled me by their devotion," and Lālūbhaṭṭa (CE 1632-1682) explains this subservience of deity to devotee by citing the distinguishing feature of "*puṣṭi*" stated by Vallabha in his *Bhāgavatārtha* 5.26: "when a devotee is dependent on Kṛṣṇa, it is the state in which the scriptural law is upheld (*maryāda*); however, when Kṛṣṇa becomes dependent on the devotee, it is an expression of grace or *puṣṭi* which supersedes all scriptural conventions."[21] In his auto-commentary on this verse (*prakāśa*), Vallabha further explains that "*puṣṭi* is thus a divine engagement, where a devotee is independent, and the supreme Lord acts in accordance with the wish of his devotee."[22] The *gopikās* are often stated as an archetype of this highest order of devotion, which begins, sustains, and culminates only through

18 Ibid, 33-34.

19 *yamevaiṣa vṛṇute tena labhyas tasyaiṣa ātmā vivṛṇute tanūṁ svām*; See S. Radhakrishnan, *The Principal Upaniṣads* (Noida: HarperCollins Publishers, 2014), 619. This is a commonly quoted Upaniṣadic verse by the classical commentators of Vallabha's treatises to explain the concept of grace (*puṣṭi*) in the philosophy of *Śuddhādvaita*. For instance, Gokulnātha, the grandson of Vallabha and a prominent commentator of his sect, quotes this verse while commenting on one of Vallabha's sixteen treatises, *Puṣṭipravāhamaryāda*, See *Ṣoḍaśagranthāḥ*, edited by Shyam M. Goswami (Bombay: Śrī Vallabhācārya Trust, 1980), 8. Vallabha's eldest son, Gopīnātha, too quotes this verse in his only available work, *Sādhanadīpikā*; See *Puṣṭividhānam*, edited by Shyam M. Goswami (Gujarat: Śrī Vallabhācārya Trust, 2004), 92; and it occurs in *Śrī-Bālakṛṣṇa-Granthāvalī*, a work by another significant author-commentator of Vallabha's sect, Lālūbhaṭṭa, see *Prameyaratnārṇava of Śrī Bālakṛṣṇa Bhaṭṭa*, trans. Kedaranatha Mishra (Anand Prakashan, 1971), 44.

20 *Ṣoḍaśagranthāḥ*, edited by Shyam M. Goswami (Bombay: Śrī Vallabhācārya Trust, 1980), 35.

21 Lālūbhaṭṭa, *Prameyaratnārṇava of Śrī Bālakṛṣṇa Bhaṭṭa*, trans. K. Mishra (Varanasi: Anand Prakashan, 1971), 89-90.

22 Vallabhācārya, *Bhāgavatārtha*, edited by Shyam M. Goswami (Kolhapur: Śrī Vallabhavidyāpīṭha-Śrī Viṭṭhaleśaprabhucaraṇāśrma Trust, 1983), 354.

the divine grace, which Vallabha titles as *śuddha-puṣṭi-bhakti*. While explaining the context of grace and grace-filled devotees, Vallabha states that these devotees of undiluted love are extremely rare (*śuddhāpremṇati-durlabhā*). Here, Puruṣottama explains the term "*śuddha*" as a form of unmediated love (*nirupādhika-prema*) and illustrates it through several episodes from the *Bhāgavata* that describe the love of the *gopikās* for Kṛṣṇa.[23] Thus, we find that on one hand, the concept of "*puṣṭi*" asserts the absolute supremacy of the divine will over the individual self, while on the other hand, the undiluted grace-filled devotion asserts the absolute accessibility of the supreme Lord to the devotee. As we have seen, Vallabha views the entire creation as a cosmic play of Brahman, where Brahman functions as both the redeemer and the redeemed, since Brahman and the finite world are not metaphysically nondifferent. This ontological presupposition is restated in the soteriology by defining the supreme Lord as the one who possesses the contrary attributes of being absolutely sovereign over, and lovingly accessible to, the devotee at the same time.

In conclusion, I posit that Vallabha's conceptualisation of *puṣṭi-bhakti* emphasises the supremacy of the Lord, and yet advocates devotion as an intensely affective relationship between two loving partners who equally crave for each other's affection. He proclaims the ascendancy of divine grace on the spiritual pilgrimage of the embodied self, and simultaneously acknowledges the loving submission of the divine Lord to the emotive affectivities of the devotee. I view this theocentric orientation as shaping Vallabha's shift from being a Vedāntic expounder of the doctrine of Brahman to an ardent Kṛṣṇa devotee whilst constructing his ritual praxis. This devotional theism both equips the devotee with the independence to employ the rich particularities of the emotions in their devotional expressions, and also curbs the manifestation of individual egoism (*ahaṃkāra*) by grounding them in the humble submission to the divine will. Hence, Vallabha juxtaposes the definition of divine grace with the idea of undiluted devotion that holds the power to control the supreme Lord, and thus, paints a picture of a supreme Lord who can be both adored as the distant sovereign and loved as the intimate beloved. The *gopikās* of Vraja are seen by Vallabha as the epitome and the ideal of this loving and coequal union between the divine grace of the supreme Lord and the unswerving, unconditional affectivity of a devotee. The *rāsapañcādhyāyī* of the *Bhāgavata*,

23 *Ṣoḍaśagranthāḥ*, edited by Shyam M. Goswami (Bombay: Śrī Vallabhācārya Trust, 1980), 52-53.

for Vallabha thus marks the climactic height of this divine devotional drama while bringing out the spectrum of theological emotivity and the ultimate fruition that a devotee achieves. In the next section, I will explore hermeneutics that Vallabha employs to understand the *rāsapañcādhyāyī* in accordance with the thematic structure of the *Bhāgavata*, which is aesthetically reflected by Nandadāsa in his poetics.

## 1.2 Theo-aesthetics of *Bhāgavata* and its Vedāntic Underpinning

The *Bhāgavata* is a concretely structured and densely woven theological text devoted to Kṛṣṇa *bhakti*, which is a theme expressed in the different *rasas* of dramaturgy.[24] While the attempts to date the *Bhāgavata* have been inconclusive so far,[25] the text itself proclaims its timeless origin to the supreme Lord Nārāyaṇa, who rendered it to the creator God Brahmā, in a condensed form of four verses (*catuḥ-ślokī Bhāgavata*). Thereupon, we find a descending line of interlocuters, through which the text gradually evolves until we reach Vyāsa, who elaborates it to the present format of twelve cantos. For the theological worldviews focused on Kṛṣṇa worship, this spatio-temporal infinity of the *Bhāgavata* establishes its divine authority much like the Vedas, and its overarching theme of devotion to Kṛṣṇa themes provides the framework for theo-aesthetics of Kṛṣṇa worship. Along with the classical theologians, the *Bhāgavata's* association with theo-aesthetics is also widely noticed in the modern scholarship. For instance, G. Schweig writes that it represents the finest imageries and poetic renditions of the "Kṛṣṇa-Gopī" love themes,[26] and while highlighting the dramaturgical aspects of the text, Wulff too states that Kṛṣṇa's seemingly human actions are more appropriately seen as instances of divine "playacting".[27] The text itself opens with an invitation to "savour

24 *Rasa* is a concept associated with Indian aesthetics which connotes emotional response that a piece of visual, literary, or performing arts evokes in an audience. The *Nāṭyaśāstra*, a classical encyclopaedic treatise on Indian performing arts, dedicates an entire section (chapter six) to elaborate this concept.

25 Scholars generally accept dates from 500 to 1000 BCE as a probable range. See E. Bryant, "The Date and Provenance of the Bhāgavata Purāṇa and the Vaikunṭha Perumāl Temple," *Journal of Vaiṣṇava Studies* 11, no. 1 (Virginia: Deepak Heritage Books, 2002), 76.

26 Graham M. Schweig, *Dance of Divine Love* (Princeton: Princeton University Press, 2005), 14.

27 Donna M. Wulff, "Drama as a Mode of Religious Realization: The Vidagdhamādhava of Rūpa Gosvāmī," *AAR Academy Series*, 43 (California: Scholars Press, 1984), 10.

the *rasa* of the *Bhāgavata*"[28] and ends by proclaiming that the one who is thus satiated by the nectar of the *Bhāgavata* will not be delighted by anything else.[29] The *Bhāgavata* also firmly emphasises its grounding in and affiliation to the Vedic truth at two crucial framing junctures – it begins with the phrase "*janmādyasya yataḥ,*"[30] which is a direct quote from the *Brahmasūtras* (1.1.2) that speak of Brahman as the foundational cause of the universe, and the text concludes by proclaiming that it contains the gist of all the Vedas.[31] Thus, the *Bhāgavata* consists of a strong thematic interweaving of Vedāntic and aesthetic concepts throughout its cantos and delineates two significant conceptual layers of cosmological-theological inquiry and devotional-aesthetic experience. Firstly, as T.S. Rukumani has noted, the *Bhāgavata* is the gospel of *bhakti* that preaches the highest form of unconditional devotion.[32] Secondly, the *Bhāgavata* articulates Kṛṣṇa as the Supreme Brahman who is completely aware of his divine identity and yet sportingly enacts diverse roles as a human being who is going through a gamut of some quotidian emotions.

The influence of the *Bhāgavata* is so profound in the Vallabhite tradition that the text itself is considered to be the literary form of Lord Kṛṣṇa, while the purpose of the life and mission of Vallabha is stated to bring forth its concealed essence. Thus, the composition of *Subodhinī* is seen as the fulfilment of this purpose, which although incomplete, is one of the most comprehensive commentaries on the *Bhāgavata*. Further, the *Bhāgavatārtha*, the third part of his exhaustive trilogy, provides a chapter-wise gist of the text. The two commentaries bring out the seven meanings of the *Bhāgavata*, of which the first four, namely, the meaning of the text as a whole (*śāstrārtha*); the meaning of the cantos (*skandhārtha*); the meaning of the tractates (*prakaraṇārtha*), and the meaning of the individual chapters (*adhyāyārtha*), is covered in the *Bhāgavatārtha*. The last three, namely, the meaning of each sentence (*vākyārtha*), each word (*śabdārtha*), and each syllable (*akśarārtha*), is elaborated in the *Subodhinī,* making it a more extensive work. As Vallabha's exegeses of the *Bhāgavata* form a comprehensive treatise which is beyond the scope of this book to explore, I will

28 *The Bhāgavata Purāṇa*: 1.1.3 (henceforth, BP).

29 BP:12.13.15

30 BP:1.1.1

31 BP:12.13.15

32 T.S. Rukumani, *A Critical Study of the Bhāgavata Purāṇa* (Varanasi: Chaukhamba Sanskrit Series, 1970), 5.

focus on those sections of his commentary which engage with the motif of the 10th canto and the quintet of the round dance.

## 1.3 *Rāsapañcādhyāyī* - The Dance of the Self with the Supreme

The *Bhāgavata's* association with the vocabularies, affectivities, and imageries of *rasa* has been extensively studied by several Indological scholars.[33] A common theme in the *bhakti* movements, thus shaped by the *Bhāgavata*, is the foregrounding of purified experiences of mundane emotions (*bhāva*) as pivotal to the processes of devotional worship, and this emphasis on a transfigured affectivity sets them apart from the world-renouncing and itinerant ascetic pathways (*saṃnyāsa*) that propound the overcoming of all worldly emotional engagements. Everyday human emotions are enriched with the incorporation of *rasa* that transforms them into aesthetic expressions of devotional love. This brings us to the two densely interwoven ideas which are at the centre of Sanskritic aesthetic theory, *bhāva* and *rasa*. While they are sometimes used interchangeably to mean emotions, the difference between them is crucial to the aesthetic theory of the *Nāṭyaśāstra* and also to the understanding of the devotional aesthetics of Vallabha. The word *rasa*, mentioned in the Upaniṣads, has a wide range of meanings.[34] However, here I will explore its definition in connection with the *bhāvas* as elucidated in the *Nāṭyaśāstra*, which speaks of eight types of *rasas* in connection with the eight permanent *sthāyībhāvas*. It is noteworthy that the term *sthāyībhāva* is understood in different ways. For instance, G.C.O. Haas proposes the word "permanent" to translate *sthāyī* and understands *bhāvas* literally as "states,"[35] while M. Ghosh understands *bhāvas* as "psychological states" and translates *sthāyī* as durable.[36] The precise relation between *bhāva* and *rasa* is itself highly debated, especially by the classical commentators such as Abhinavagupta and Bhoja – while

33 For instance, see Ithamar Theodor's "The Pariṇāma Aesthetics as Underlying the Bhāgavata Purāṇa," *Asian Philosophy: An International Journal of the Philosophical Traditions of the East* 17, no. 2, (Routledge, 2007).

34 Daniel Meyer-Dinkgräfe's *Approaches to Acting: Past and Present* (London: Continuum, 2005), 102-103 and *Consciousness, Theatre, Literature and the Arts 2011*, edited by Daniel Meyer-Dinkgräfe (Newcastle upon Tyne: Cambridge Scholars Publishing, 2012), 243.

35 G.C.O. Haas, *The Daśarūpa, A Treatise on Hindu Dramaturgy by Dhanaṁjaya* (Delhi: Motilal Banarasidass, 1962), 106-129.

36 *Nāṭyaśāstram* – Vol. 1, edited by Manmohan Ghosh (Calcutta: Manish Granthālaya, 1967), 102.

the former states that *rasa* transcends the ordinary *bhāva*, the latter emphasises that the aesthetic enjoyment of *rasa* is just a further development of *bhāva*.[37] In the *Nāṭyaśāstra*, *rati* (passionate love) is the *sthāyībhāva* of *śṛṅgāra-rasa* (mood of passion). However, *bhāva* for Vallabha is neither the *sthāyībhāva* nor the *rasa* of the *Nāṭyaśāstric* description. Giving an entirely theocentric meaning to the term, Vallabha defines *bhāva* as an experience of an emotional state when God becomes the supreme object of love (*rati*). Hence, I argue that the efflorescence of *bhāva* in Vallabha's theology is expressed as *bhakti*.[38] Further, while Bhoja takes *śṛṅgāra-rasa* to be the supreme *rasa*, Abhinavagupta defends the supremacy of *śānta-rasa*. As we have seen, the dramatic nature of the *Bhāgavata* is widely recognised, and it is possible to read it through the lens of *śṛṅgāra-rasa* or *śānta-rasa*. However, for Vallabha such a disjunctive reading would be specious as the former would merely explore the passions of love without acknowledging Brahman's paramountcy and the latter would limit itself to the knowledge of Brahman while disregarding the playful duality *līlātmika-dvaita*) between the deity and the devotee. As we shall see, the devotional-aesthetic (*bhakti-rasa*) reading of the *Bhāgavata* provides the synthesis of both, a duality that incorporates the mood of passion and a non-duality that incorporates the mood of quietude. This blissful co-existence of playful duality with ontological non-duality is the crux of Vallabha's philosophy of "Pure Non-dualism" (*Śuddhādvaita*).

Quoting the *Bṛhadāraṇyaka Upaniṣad*, Vallabha comments that the entire cosmos comes into being as an expression of the supreme reality's delightful play (*ramaṇa*) which is only possible to express in, and through, a world of diversity.[39] J.R. Timm explains this motif of world-production as a form of the self-forgetfulness of the supreme self for the manifestation of diversity as God separates "himself" from "himself."[40] This pure love is the basis of all aesthetic moods.[41] Thus *bhakti-rasa* is the sentiment of love that is generated through the knowledge of the interweaving of ontological

37 David L. Haberman, *Acting as a Way of Salvation: A Study of Rāgānugā Bhakti Sādhanā* (New York: Oxford University Press, 2001), 27.

38 *Śāstrārtha*:42; See *Tatvārtha-dīpa-nibandha*, edited by Shyam M. Goswami (Kolhapur: Śrīvallabhavidyāpīṭha-Śrīviṭṭhaleśaprabhucaraṇāśrma Trust, 1982), 68-70.

39 *Śāstrārtha*:23; See *Tatvārtha-dīpa-nibandha*, edited by Shyam M. Goswami (Kolhapur: Śrīvallabhavidyāpīṭha-Śrīviṭṭhaleśaprabhucaraṇāśrma Trust, 1982), 61.

40 Jeffrey R. Timm, "Prolegomenon to Vallabha's Theology of Revelation," *Philosophy of East and West* 38, no. 2 (University of Hawai'i Press, 1988), 116.

41 *Subodhinī*:1.19.16, (Bombay: Gujarati Publication, 1986), 291.

non-duality and playful duality; the former is cognised as the supreme knowledge of one unifying principleal[42] and the latter is embraced as the volitional submission to the divine will which is manifesting as many.[43] Hence, R. Chaudhury describes the devotion of the Vallabha tradition as the sweetest, softest, and purest form of *bhakti* (*mādhurya-pradhāna-bhakti*) which involves intimate, personal relations between the deity and the devotee as "two equal partners."[44] When complete awareness of non-duality is expressed with unmotivated love, self-delightment becomes the core feature of the devotion. Non-duality in Vallabha's philosophy therefore does not limit the scope of devotion but is the very feature which separates the mood of *bhakti* from all the other moods.

While the *Bhāgavata* continuously speaks about cultivating devotion to Kṛṣṇa,[45] the detailed narratives of Kṛṣṇa only begin in the 10th Canto. It is not a coincidence that this canto is the longest one and is also dominated by the accounts of Kṛṣṇa's playful acts. The thematic categorisation of the *Bhāgavata*, especially of the 10th Canto, which is by far considered to be the most significant amongst the Kṛṣṇa-*bhakti* traditions, has largely been disputed. Notwithstanding the text's own thematic delineation of its cantos, some traditional commentators propose to switch the themes of the 10th Canto, namely, *nirodha*, with that of the 12th Canto, namely *āśraya* (*Tattva-sandarbha*: 59.4).[46] One of the strongest arguments provided for this variation is that *nirodha* as per the *Bhāgavata*'s definition is "the slumber of the supreme Lord", and thus, it actually points towards the involution or the end of the cosmic creation. Hence, if *nirodha* is accepted to be the theme of the 10th Canto, it would make the next two cantos redundant. On the other hand, *āśraya*, the theme of the 12th Canto, invariably points to Kṛṣṇa, the eternal refuge of the individual self, as the supreme feature of the entire 10th Canto. Thus, it is proposed that if the themes of the 10th and the 12th Canto are switched, it amounts to a more coherent understanding of the

42 *Chāndogya Upaniṣad* 6.2.1.

43 *Chāndogya Upaniṣad* 6.2.3

44 Roma Chaudhuri, *Ten Schools Of The Vedānta,* Part 1 (Calcutta: Rabindra Bharti University, 1973), 143.

45 For instance, Ravi Gupta and Kenneth Valpey write that even the word "Bhāgavata" means related to Bhagavān, the Blessed Lord, and this word primarily refers to the devotees of Kṛṣṇa. Ravi M. Gupta and Kenneth R. Valpey, "Churning the Ocean of Līlā: Themes for Bhāgavata Study," *The Bhāgavata Purāṇa* (New York: Columbia University Press, 2013), 2.

46 See Jīva Gosvāmī's *Śrī Tattvasandarbha*, edited by H. Shastri (Mathura: Śrī Gadādharagaurahari Press, 1983), 155-160.

text and its structural motifs.[47] Disagreeing with the altered classification, Vallabha strongly supports the original categorisation by the *Bhāgavata* in his commentary. He elaborates the definition of *āśraya* as a state of final fruition of devotion, when the supreme refuge is attained, which invariably marks the end of both devotional and cosmic journey of a devotee. Quoting the *Taittirīya Upaniṣad* (3.1) to support his argument, Vallabha states that in the aforementioned Upaniṣadic verse, "that from which every existing object originates"[48] denotes the first two themes of the text; and "that by which they subsists"[49] denotes the subsequent eight themes; while "that towards which they move and merge"[50] denotes the ninth theme; and finally, "that Brahman"[51] denotes the final theme of *āśraya*. In this way, *āśraya* is said to be the conclusive final refuge of cosmos, which is elucidated in the 12th Canto, while the playful engagement of the supreme Lord in the 10th Canto correlates to his concealment of divinity in order to enjoy the devotion of the *gopikās*, as elaborated earlier.

The central theme of this canto, namely, *nirodha* (constraint),[52] needs to be properly understood before we proceed to the discussion of *rāsa* in this canto.[53] The *Bhāgavata* defines *nirodha* as the slumber (*anuśayana*) of the blessed Lord with all his powers.[54] Vallabha reads the word *anuśayana*

---

47 See S.M. Elkman's *Jīva Gosvāmin's Tattvasandarbha* (Delhi: Motilal Banarasidass, 1986), 63-165.

48 "*Yato vā imāni bhūtāni jāyante*" marks the beginning of the creation and hence is taken to underline the primary creation (*sarga*) and secondary creation (*visarga*).

49 "*yena jātāni jīvanti*" marks the sustenance and gradual evolution of cosmos, and it thus marks the cosmic situation (*sthāna*), graceful nourishment (*poṣaṇa*), impetus for fruitive action (*ūti*), the righteous reigns of Manus (*manvantara*), stories of the devotees (*īśānukathā*), and the slumber of divine powers (*nirodha*).

50 "*yatprayantya abhisaṁviśanti*" marks the final dissolution and is thus taken to underline the theme of liberation (*mukti*).

51 "*tad brahmeti*" is the noun that is defined by the aforementioned characteristics, which is denoted in the final canto of the *Bhāgavata* in a similar fashion. Thus, *āśraya* is taken to be the noun that is characterised by the first nine themes.

52 The *Bhāgavata* while delineating the themes of its Cantos declares *nirodha* to be the theme of the 10th Canto (2.10.1)

53 Kṛṣṇa-*bhakti* traditions in the region of Braja combine the aesthetic definitions of *rasa* originated from the *Nāṭyaśāstra* with the Upaniṣadic idea of "Brahman itself is rasa" (*raso vai saha*; *Tattirīya Upaniṣad* 2.7.1) and construct theo-aesthetics of *rasa*, which is defined as the devotional emotivities evoked by the stories of Kṛṣṇa found in the text of the *Bhāgavata*. The *bhakti* traditions of Vallabha and Caitanya prominently use this theme to build their devotional orthopraxis that closely follows the affectivities of *gopikās*.

54 BP:2.10.6

metaphorically as the playful repose of the Lord and articulates two aspects of the word *nirodha*. Firstly, Kṛṣṇa, who is the supreme reality of the world, descends to the world by constraining his power to engage in playacting.[55] Thus, *nirodha* is Kṛṣṇa constraining his supernatural cosmic play into the finite structures of the material world. Secondly, this constraint is not directionless for it is shaped by the goal of the salvation of his devotees. This second aspect of *nirodha* is established when Kṛṣṇa through his plays attracts the embodied selves in a way that they forget the material world (*prapañcavismṛti*) and become passionately attached to him (*bhagavadāsakti*) (*Bhāgavatārtha*; 10.15). Thus, the first definition speaks of the transcendental nature, whilst the second describes the soteriological effect of *nirodha*. Vallabha further describes *nirodha* both as the means (*sādhanā*) and as the effect (*phala*). The former is characterised by the Lord's descent for soteriological playacting (*līlā*) that is reciprocated by the devotee's yearning, and the latter is characterised by the devotee's involvement in the divine play. As F. Smith notes, *nirodha* is both the cessation of ordinary reality and the actualisation of the highest state of *bhakti* by integration into Kṛṣṇa's divine play.[56] This state of *bhakti* is described as *bhajanānanda* (bliss of worshipping) as opposed to *brahmānanda* (bliss of attaining oneness with the impersonal Brahman). As Vallabha's commentary carefully follows the thematic structures of the *Bhāgavata*, it is designed to highlight the specific themes of the Canto in each of its ninety chapters. Thus, to understand the *pañcādhyāyī* – the five chapters that celebrate the *rāsa* dance – in the light of Vallabha's commentary, it is fundamental to place it within the framework of *nirodha*. Nandadāsa's poetic rendition of this quintet is thematically underpinned by these theological ideas of the Vallabhite tradition.

The five chapters of the *pañcādhyāyī* sequentially illustrate the arrival of the *gopikās* in the dance; the disappearance of Kṛṣṇa and the anguish of the *gopikās*; the song of separation; Kṛṣṇa's reappearance and reassurance; and the climactic final dance. Of these, the first chapter begins with the call of Kṛṣṇa's flute, hearing which the *gopikās* embark towards the forest. However, when a few of them see the male members of their families on the doorstep, they are unable leave the house. These *gopikās*, known as the

55 *Bhāgavatārtha*:10.14b-15a. See *Bhāgavatārtha* – Vol. 2, edited by Shaym M. Goswami (Jodhpur: Sri Subodhinī Prakāśana Maṇḍal, 1971), 4.

56 Frederick Smith, "Nirodha And The Nirodhalakṣaṇa Of Vallabhācārya," *Journal of Indian Philosophy* 26 (1998), 499.

*antaḥ-gṛha-gataḥ* (those who stayed in the house), then meditate on the divine form of Kṛṣṇa and eventually merge their selves with the supreme Self of the supreme Lord (*brahmānanda*). The *Bhāgavata* states that these *gopikās* loved Kṛṣṇa with an erotic desire (*jārabhāva*), and yet achieved the highest form of liberation through their final act of austere meditative worship.[57] Vallabha marks this passage as a crucially significant one, for it defines the characteristics of the dance as well as that of Kṛṣṇa and the *gopikās*. He explains that if these *gopikās* had cognised the essential form of Kṛṣṇa as the supreme Self, their arrival would not have been hindered. It is the erotic love for Kṛṣṇa that obstructs their understanding of his essential form and ultimately leads to their exclusion from the dance.[58] In contrast, the *gopikās* who manage to arrive are the ones who have conceived Kṛṣṇa as the all-encompassing transcendental nondual Brahman (*advaita*), who is simultaneously the profoundly passible and the supremely personal God (*dvaita*). Here, the awareness of duality serves the purpose of divine play (*ramaṇa*); sublating it with ontological non-duality, in the form of an undifferentiated union, would go against the divine will of manifestation. Conversely, overlooking the essential non-dualism atrophies the devotion into moods which are stamped with material imperfection, such as *jārabhāva*. The *gopikās* who are able to arrive in the dance are thus traditionally viewed as the personified forms of the Vedic hymns (*śrutirūpā*). Summing up the essence of this dance, Dikṣita Gosvāmī (CE) states that in his final chapters of the *Brahmasūtras*, Vyāsa synthesizes the variegated contrasts of the *śruti* verses in Brahman, defining it the abode of all contrasts. This process is achieved through epistemological hermeneutics of the scriptural texts. Similarly, in the *pañcādhyāyī*, Vyāsa attempts to do the same through the personification of the *śrutis* in the form of *gopikās* and Brahman in the form of Kṛṣṇa. The only difference is that here, the synthesis is achieved through the loving act of devotional worship.[59] Vallabha explains that this oneness is far greater than the non-dual merger of the yogis' selves with Brahman, for even in their mental embrace, the *gopīkās* have experienced the amalgamation of all the *rasas* through all their sense-organs and reached the pinnacle of *bhakti-rasa*. This summit is a paradoxical state where even the blessed Lord becomes indebted to the devotee.

57 The *Bhāgavata*, 10.29.9-11.

58 Vallabhācārya, *Rāsapañcādhyāyī Śrī Subodhinī*, trans. Pandit J. Caturvedī (Varanasi: Chaukhambha Bharati Academy, 2017), 44.

59 Ibid, 7-10.

Thus, Vallabha's theology culminates with the soteriological paradox in which it is God who submits to the devotee's love, and the devotee values the joy of remaining bound to *saṃsāra* as God's blessed servant (*bhajanānanda*) over that of being liberated by attaining an undifferentiated oneness with the supreme self (*brahmānanda*).

As we now understand the theological underpinning of Nandadāsa's poetic rendition, we proceed towards an introduction to *Havelī-Saṅgīta*, which is a systematic music tradition of *Puṣṭimārga*, established by the compositions of the eight devotional poets collectively known as the *aṣṭa-chāpas*. Nandadāsa is one of these *aṣṭa-chāpas*, and it is significant to cognize the nuance details of this devotional music tradition to fully understand this work.

TWO

# *Aṣṭa-Chāpa* - Their Origin and the Legacy

MUSIC HAS BEEN an instrumental part of worship and liturgy in various Hindu traditions since the earliest times. Sound in its primordial form (*nāda*) is seen as the core of the creation (*Muṇḍaka Upaniṣad*: 2.2.8),[60] and thus, thc musical link to the supreme Self is a well-explored phenomenon of Indian studies. The compositions of Nandadāsa, including the *rāsapañcādhyāyī* are a part of both the theological and sonic legacy of the devotional music of *Puṣṭimārga*, which was later known as *Havelī Saṅgīta*. It derives its name from the traditional homes (*havelī*) of the descendants of Vallabha, where it was customarily rendered in the devotional service of the deity that resided within. This musical legacy of *Puṣṭimārga* was first founded by the group of eight poet-devotees (*aṣṭa-chāpa*) who offered their services at the original temple of Śrīnāthajī atop mount Govardhana, which later became a centre for the Kṛṣṇa-*bhakti* traditions of Braja. Such liturgical, devotional, and philosophical interweaving of music can be found since its very onset. Although there exists little documented information about the kinds of music in the Vedic age, it is traditionally believed that it was developed for both secular (*laukika*) and sacred (Vedic) purposes. The genesis of music in India and the historical timeline of its development is a comprehensive subject that is beyond the scope of this work. Hence, here I will only highlight the foundation of some of the key elements of devotional music in India that directly influence the musical structure of *Havelī Saṅgīta* and Nandadāsa's poetry.

60 R. Hume, *The Thirteen Principal Upanishads* (England: Oxford University Press, 1921), 27-36.

## 2.1 The Emergence of Devotional Music in India

The earliest instance of systematised music can be found in the *Sāmaveda*, namely the *sāma-gāna*, which essentially consists of the hymns of the *Ṛgveda* that are tuned into a set of musical patterns and notes progressing in a descending order. *Sāma-gāna* steadily evolved from using a four-notes scale to a seven-notes scale with elaborate meters (*chanda*) and development of repetitive musical cycle (*āvaratana*). Some of its characteristic features constitute the rudimentary structure of Indian music even in the present times. For instance, the involvement of elongated vowels (*stobhas*), which are basically meaningless syllables used as a prologue to establish the main melody, gave rise to the concept of *ālāpa* that serves as the opening section of the Indian classical music, especially *dhrupad*. In the words of Guy L. Beck, a prominent musicologist, music was an invisible link to the ritual of Vedic sacrifice through the system of merit accumulation.[61] He quotes the study of S. McIntosh, who mentions *gandharva* as a generic term for all formalised music, which was valued as secondary Veda.[62] This *gandharva* music included the components of *svara* (tone), *tāla* (beat), and *pada* (word) rendered as per the set rules to gain various spiritual fruits.

Invariably, the divine origin of music is often traced to the gods, who created it for celestial pleasure, and the knowledge was then passed on to the humans by the sage of the gods, Nārada. Perhaps this is why the rudimentary principles of ancient Indian music are known as *gandharva-saṅgīta*, named after the celestial musicians (*gandharvas*). The word *saṅgīta*, which is a common term for music in many Indian languages, includes a triad of vocal, instrumental, and dance. One of the first systematic accounts on these musical principles can be found in the *Nāṭyaśāstra* and the *Dattilam* (both 300 BCE), of which the former is primarily dedicated to the theatre arts and the latter is credited with the systematic categorisation of the basic musical structure, namely the *jātis*. The *Dattilam* also marks the transition in Indian music from *sāma-gāna* to *gandharva-saṅgīta*, as the latter then became the raw material for both sacred and secular music

61 Guy L. Beck's "Two Braja Bhāṣā Versions of the Rāsa-Līlā Pancādhyāyī and Their Musical Performance in Vaiṣṇava Worship," *The Bhāgavata Purāṇa: Sacred Text and Living Tradition*, edited by Ravi M. Gupta and Kenneth R. Valpey (New York: Columbia University Press, 2013), 182.

62 Solveig McIntosh, *Hidden Faces of Ancient Indian Song* (Burlington: Ashgate Publishing, 2005), 79.

in the Indian subcontinent. The roots of the two major schools of music in India, namely, the Hindustani Classical from the north and the Carnatic from the south, can be found in principles mentioned in these texts.

Another critical classical Sanskrit work on music, *Bṛhaddeśi* (c.a. 6th-8th CE) by sage Mātaṅga, was instrumental in systematising the concept of *rāga* (melodic mode) and introducing the notion of *saragama* (notations or *sol-fa*), both of which continue to be key concepts in Indian music. Mātaṅga first distinguished between *mārgi* music (classical) and *deśi* music (regional), of which the former was sacred in nature while the latter was secular music created by the common folk for their enjoyment.[63] This brings us to the era of *Saṅgīta Ratnākara* (13th Century) by Śārṅgāradeva, which is considered a text of categorical significance in the development of both the Hindustani Classical and the Carnatic music. This text reaffirmed the distinction between *mārgi* and *deśi* music by highlighting the adherence of *mārgi* music to the classical principles of the *Nātyaśāstra* while the *deśi* music attuned itself to the regional improvisations. The steady sophistication of *deśi* music led to the formation of *prabandha* compositions, which were both the precursors to the emergence of devotional music in India and had a deep connection with the musical legacy of the *rāsapañcādhyāyī*. Although the word "*prabandha*" is simply defined by Mātaṅga as "that which is composed", the distinctness of *prabandhas* lies in the keen focus given to the poetics of its compositions. This phenomenon finds its way in *dhrupad*, which is also known for the emphasis given to its poetics, and later into *Havelī Saṅgīta* that goes a step ahead in giving primacy to its poetry over music. While Mātaṅga explained *deśi* music with 48 varieties of *prabandhas*, Śārṅgāradeva divided it into 77 categories with more than 4200 sub-variations.[64]

The complicated journey of *prabandha* music cannot be discussed here in detail; however, two of its categories, namely, *śuddha-sūḍa-prabandha* and *sālaga-sūḍa-prabandha*, are important musical styles connected to the *Bhāgavata-bhakti* traditions. As Emmie te Nijenhuis notes in her work on the *Dattilam*, both these *prabandhas* included *dhruva* songs

63 Ashok D. Ranade, *Music Contexts: A Concise Dictionary of Hindustani Music* (New Delhi: Promilla and Co. Publishers, 2006), 199-200.

64 Mātaṅga, too, accepts that *prabandhas*, in reality, are countless and their complexities cannot be grasped by everyone Śārṅgāradeva lays out in chapter four of *Saṁgītaratnākara*. See Pandit S.S. Sāstrī's *Saṁgītaratnākara* - Vol. II, (Chennai: The Adyar Library and Research Centre, 1959), 203-349.

from the *Nāṭyaśāstra*,[65] which were originally compositions dedicated to emotions and ecstasy. These musical nuances are undeniably significant in the context of *rāsapañcādhyāyī*, as the *Bhāgavata* (10.33) itself mentions intricate knowledge of music that the *gopikās* possessed. Even the later authors, in their retelling of this *Bhāgavata* episode, mention the elaborate musical details including the subtleties and sheer variety of singing styles, instruments, and dance that was used in this divine musical saga. For instance, the *Ānanda Vṛndāvana* by Kavi Karṇapūra from the Gauḍiya Vaiṣṇava tradition is a fine example of Sanskrit poetic rendition that mentions the details of music, dance, and instruments used by the *gopikās*, and especially worth noting here is the reference to *dhruva* songs and the rendition of *śuddha-prabandha*.[66] Thus, a comprehensive reading of the *rāsapañcādhyāyī* cannot be completed without the inclusion of the finer musical elements that are incorporated in its original, as well as in the later retellings. These *dhruva* songs, commonly composed in Prākṛta dialects, were categorised by the *Nāṭyaśāstra* on the basis of the superiority of their emotional quality (3.24-25).[67] As none of these songs survived their original compositions, in the post-*Nāṭyaśāstra* period they were recomposed in the *prabandha* style leading to the birth of *dhruva-prabandha*, which became the forerunner of *dhruvapada* or as it now known, *dhrupad*. As S. Thielemann notes in her work on the music in the Vaiṣṇava temples, *dhruvapada* is most likely to be the principal type of composition in Vaiṣṇava devotional singing, and the interpretation of *dhruva* as *dhruvapada* indeed gains authority in this context.[68]

## 2.2 The Era of *Dhrupad* and the Rise of Regional Saint-poets

*Dhrupad* or *dhruvapada* can be loosely translated as "immovable verse," referring to the set of structured songs that initially formed most of its compositions. When it was later popularised as courtly format of musical rendition, *dhrupad* became a term associated with both the form of poetry

65 Emmie te Nijenhuis, *Dattilam: A Compedium of Ancient Indian Music* (Leiden: E.J. Brill, 1970), 370.

66 Karṇapūra, *Ānanda Vṛndāvana Campū*, (The University of Michigan Press, 1999), 327.

67 *Nāṭyaśāstram* – Vol. 2, edited by Manmohan Ghosh (Calcutta: Manish Granthālaya, 1967), 880-900.

68 Selina Thielemann, *The Music of South Asia* (The University of Michigan Press, 1999), 357.

and the style of its musical composition. Although the compositions depicted themes like romance, eulogy, philosophy, and royal panegyrics, it primarily gained popularity for its devotional compositions when it was revived in the late 15th and 16th centuries by the *bhakti* saints of Braja region, including the poets of the Vallabha tradition. Contextually, the most crucial reference for both the history and devotional relevance of *dhrupad* occurs in the *Bhāgavata* (10.33.10), when the *gopikās* render a *dhrupad* melody during the celebrated round dance with Kṛṣṇa. I argue as *dhrupad* was used by Kṛṣṇa's most adored devotees to please him, its popularity is invariably enhanced amongst the devotional saints, making it a highly preferred style for devotional compositions, especially in the *Kṛṣṇa-bhakti* traditions. Retaining the original spirit of the *dhruvas, dhrupad* songs are known for their emotive quality and the use of vernacular languages, which is also a factor leading to their popularity in the *Bhāgavata-bhakti* circles. The rich musical heritage of the *Bhāgavata*, primarily constituting the *kīrtana* (devotional songs), is known for its use of the folk language and the employment of cymbals (*jhānjha*) to mark the rhythmic movement of the beats (*tāla*). G.L. Beck thoroughly examines the role of the *Bhāgavata* in popularising worship-through-music (*kīrtana-bhakti*), especially in the vernacular dialects, by pointing out that as a form of worship it is not only acknowledged but also promoted by the text (11.27.45).[69]

While eminent sitar maestro Pt Ravi Shankar states that *dhrupad* replaced the *prabandha* singing in India,[70] some of its traces were retained in the folk musical traditions such as the *Samāja Gāyana* and the *Havelī Saṅgīta*, both of which are close cousins and offshoots of *dhrupad*. As Ritwik Sanyal notes, although the earliest source of the current form of *dhrupad* is found in the *Ain-I-Akbari* of Abu Fazl (1593), much of its later evolution is attributed to the patronage of King Man Singh Tomar of Gwalior (ca. 1486-1516), who was an accomplished musician and composer of his times.[71] His court was also credited with the cultivation of *Braja-*

69 Guy L. Beck's "Two Braja Bhāṣā Versions of the Rāsa-Līlā Pancādhyāyī and Their Musical Performance in Vaiṣṇava Worship," *The Bhāgavata Purāṇa: Sacred Text and Living Tradition*, edited by Ravi M. Gupta and Kenneth R. Valpey (New York: Columbia University Press, 2013), 181-190.

70 See *Raga Mala: The Autobiography of Ravi Shankar*, edited by George Harrison (New York: Welcome Rain Publishers, 1999), 319.

71 Ritwik Sanyal and Richard Widdess, *Dhrupad: Tradition and Performance in Indian Music* – Vol. 1 (Englad: Ashgate, 2004), 45-46.

*bhāṣā*,[72] which is a regionally modified form (*apabhraṁśa*) of Prākṛta and medieval Hindi. This is contextually relevant on two accounts, firstly, *dhrupad*, *Havelī Saṅgīta*, and *samāja gāyana* were all traditionally sung in non-Sanskrit dialects, and the royal patronage of *Braja-bhāṣā* led to it dominating the bulk of the compositions of these musical forms. Especially noteworthy are the compositions of *Havelī Saṅgīta*, which are only rendered in *Braja-bhāṣā*, barring very few exceptions that are in Sanskrit. Secondly, an abundance of *Braja-bhāṣā* poetry was produced in this time, as the language gained the attention of *bhakti*-saints such as Raskhān (ca 1548-1628), *Aṣṭa-chāpas* (approx. ca. 1450-1600), Harirām Vyās (1511-1630), and others. Although Sanskrit enjoyed the status of being the divine scriptural language, according to these *bhakti*-saints in the supreme land of salvation (celestial *Vṛndāvana* or *Goloka*) Kṛṣṇa and the *gopikās* speak in their native tongue, which is *Braja-bhāṣā*. This conception gave the language a venerable position amongst the Kṛṣṇa devotional traditions, putting it on a higher plane than Sanskrit.

Another important contribution of King Man Singh Tomar was songs written in three volumes, namely, the *viṣṇupadas* (praise of Lord Viṣṇu), *dhrupads*, and *dhamār/horī* (Kṛṣṇa celebrating the festival of Holi). Of these, the *dhamār/horī* singing became a crucial element of the music of Braja and was later included into the vast corpus of *Havelī Saṅgīta* poetries. The *aṣṭa-chāpa* then developed their own *dhamār* compositions, which became the core element of the spring festival of Holi celebrated in *Puṣṭimārga*. At the same time, Tānsen (ca. 1493-1586), the pupil of Svāmī Haridās (ca. 1500-1595) of the *Nimbārka* sect, rose to fame with his *Kṛṣṇa-bhakti* compositions of *dhrupad*, which brought *dhrupad* to the Mughal court.[73] Widely regarded as the father of Hindustani Classical music, Tānsen is a central figure connected to the triad of the Gwalior court, the Mughal court, and *Puṣṭimārga*. Before he became the primary musician in the court of Akbar and found his place amongst his nine jewels (*nava-ratanas*), he was groomed by Svāmī Haridās in the Gwalior school (*gharāna*) of *dhrupad* music in the court of King Man Singh Tomar. While there are no historical accounts, the folk culture of Braja and the traditional literature of *Puṣṭimārga* also mention a profound connection between Tansen and one of the *aṣṭa-chāpas*, namely, Govindasvāmī (ca. 1505-1585), and thus,

72 *Bhavan's Journal* 33 (1986), 162.

73 Bonnie C. Wade, *Imaging Sound: An Ethnomusicological Study of Music, Art, and Culture in Mughal India* (Chicago: University of Chicago Press, 1998), 114-117.

several compositions of Tānsen were then included in *Havelī Saṅgīta*. The age of Man Singh Tomar is hence an important link in the development of both *dhrupad* in its present format and the regional music of Braja that had significant influence on the musical heritage of *Puṣṭimārga*. Further, we observe that when *dhrupad* gained prevalence as a notable musical style of the Hindustani Classical most of its famed compositions were rooted in *Kṛṣṇa-bhakti* and *Kṛṣṇa-līlā*, which established an important link between the legacy of *dhrupad* and the Vaiṣṇava devotional traditions.

Before we delve into the world of *Havelī Saṅgīta*, it is significant to note that it is an oral tradition that constantly changed and synchronised itself with the progression of music at every age. As a living tradition, its legacy was preserved over the years by various generations of practitioners who rendered it as a part of their devotional worship. The historical untraceability invariably becomes a part of a living tradition that has an oral history, and this often leads one to trace various versions presented by its followers, to analyse their daily practice, and to conceptualise it on the basis of its theological backdrop. I follow a similar process here – the information that I intend to present is largely built on the narratives of its seasoned practitioners and the understanding that I acquired over the years as an insider of this ever-evolving tradition of music and worship. For a clearer comprehension, I will classify the key concepts of *Havelī Saṅgīta* into three sections: The Structure, the Liturgical and Exegetical Value, and the Method of its Rendition.

## 2.3 The Structure of *Havelī Saṅgīta*

The *aṣṭa-chāpa* poems commonly were attributed to them by identifying the "stamp" (*chāpa*) used in the last stanza, which usually was a part or a slightly different form of their original names. Crucially, the poetries available today have been collected and penned down over the years through different sources while the musical structure of their composition was orally passed on to its practitioners. Although it is difficult to conclusively trace the extant poetries or their original compositions back to their founders, the exiting shape of *Havelī Saṅgīta* is valued, accepted, and venerated in the tradition as a surviving legacy of the great *aṣṭa-chāpa* poets and forms an indispensable part of *Puṣṭimārga*. The *Havelī Saṅgīta* has been a relatively understudied style of music in India and to a large extent the practice of this musical tradition was limited to the followers of the tradition. One of the primary reasons for its modest spread is the deliberate attempt by its founders and practitioners to keep it exclusively private due to its sacrosanct status in the tradition. The rendition of *Havelī Saṅgīta* is supposed to be a private affair between the devotee and the personal form of Kṛṣṇa that one worships, wherein the sole purpose was to cultivate unconditional devotion based on the parental love of Yaśodā or the passionate love of the *gopikās*.

Although this musical tradition was established during the period of Vallabha, it is his son and co-founder of *Puṣṭimārga*, Viṭṭhalanātha, who is traditionally credited with the expansion of the orthopraxy with the addition of offering, melody, and ornamentation, collectively known as *bhoga-rāga-śṛṅgāra*. The progression of *rāga* established an organised system of musical tradition in the old temple of Śrīnāthajī with the *aṣṭa-chāpa* posing as the chief musicians. The devotional service of this temple governed by Viṭṭhalanātha with its rich cultural heritage of devotion attracted musicians and devotees from far and wide, such as Raskhān, Tānsen, Dhondhī, Haridās, and others. *Puṣṭimārga* eventually spread westwards to Rajasthan and Gujarat, and in the 17th century the embodied form of Śrīnāthajī was shifted to its new base in Mewar, Rajasthan (Nāthadvārā) in order to safeguard it from the Mughal ruler Aurangzeb.[74] In coming years, Nāthadvārā became a new centre for *Puṣṭimārga* and its musical legacy, which then reinvented itself by adopting the folk music of this region. As the birthplace of *Havelī Saṅgīta*, Braja remained as its original school (*Mathura-gharāna*); however, in later years with the spread of *Puṣṭimārga*, four primary centres of its music were created in Rajasthan, Gujarat, Banaras, and Mumbai.[75] While each of these *gharānas* retained the original ingredients of *Havelī Saṅgīta*, the flavour of the land eloquently refined its taste. Two of the most celebrated musicians of *Havelī Saṅgīta* have been from the lineage of Vallabha, namely, Pt Mukundarāyajī Mahārāja and Pt Gokulotsavajī Mahārāja. While they were not contemporaries, their contribution in the evolution of this musical tradition is substantial and they are largely responsible for creating a wider audience for it outside of *Puṣṭimārga*. The former was known for his mastery over the string instrument *vīn*ā and credited with the revival of *dhrupad* in *Puṣṭimārga*, while the latter is the most celebrated singer of *Havelī Saṅgīta* in the modern times, holding the honour of third-highest civilian award in India (*padma-vibhūṣaṇa*) for his

74 Gopal K. Agrawal, *Changing Frontiers of Religion* (Agra Book Store: 1983), 36.

75 Pandit Mukundarāy Goswami, *Nādarasa* (Mumbai: Gīta Saṁgīta Sāgara Trust, 2012), x-xi.

contribution in music. I will employ both their opinions, although they are slightly different from each other, to build the basic structure of *Havelī Saṅgīta*.

As a traditionalist, Pt Mukundarāyaji Mahārāja passionately believed in the revival of the original *dhrupad* compositions, which faced a challenge due to the rising popularity of *khayal* singing. In his seminal work, the *Nādarasa*, he has attempted to restore the old *dhrupad-dhamār* style, which is a four-fold structural formation of *dhrupad* songs that are set to *dhamār* meter.[76] The *dhamār* and the *cautāla* are common musical meters used in the *dhrupad* songs of *Havelī Saṅgīta*, of which the former consists of 14 beats in asymmetrical pattern (5-2-3-4) and the latter is formed of 12 beats symmetrically divided in six parts. As it is known, a classic *dhrupad* song has four sections, namely, *sthāyī*, *antarā*, *sancārī*, and *abhogī*. Of these *sthāyī* operates in the middle to lower octave, *antara* uses middle to higher octave, while *sancārī* oscillates between *sthāyī* and *antarā* and synchronises them using all three octaves. Finally, the song concludes with *abhogī*, which uses the familiar notes of *sthāyī* with a slight variation. While *abhogī* ties the melody together, it is commonly accompanied by an increasing pace of the rhythmic meter (*calatī*) in the end, which goes twice as fast (*duguna*) or sometimes four times the original pace of the meter (*cauguna*). A distinctive characteristic of *calatī* in *Havelī Saṅgīta* is that while the meter increases its pace, the singing goes on at the same pace so that the words of the song do not become either incomprehensible or lose their emotivity. This emphasis on words is another feature that highlights the idea of prioritizing the poetry and its emotive essence over the musical complexity, which is sometimes referred to as *śabda-pradhāna-gāyakī* in the tradition. In his work, Pt Mukundarāyajī Mahārāja neatly incorporates all these conventional aspects of *dhrupad* with the idea of preserving their essential form. The *Nādarasa* for the most part consists of *dhrupad* songs that are set in the musical meter of *dhamār*, *cautāla*, and *jhapatāla* (10 beats: 2-3-2-3) in that order of frequency. Admitting the diversity of singing styles that were later incorporated in the tradition, he also created some of the *khayāl* compositions mostly in *tritāla* (16 beats – equal division), albeit clearly stating that *dhrupad-dhamār* will always be the foundational style that provides *Havelī Saṅgīta* its essence.

On the other hand, Pt Gokulotsavjī Mahārāja strongly advocates against compartmentalizing of *Havelī Saṅgīta* in any particular school or

76 Ibid, iii-v.

musical style and equally acknowledges the inclusion of them all. Taking a more liberal view, he states that as an ever-evolving musical tradition, the purpose of *Havelī Saṅgīta* was always to please Kṛṣṇa with the best piece of creation. In this process, popular singing styles such as *dhrupad, khayāl, ṭhumrī, ṭappā, prabandha,* and even *samāja gāyana* were interweaved together over the years of its evolution. Hence, although *dhrupad-dhamār* forms its foundational structure, *Havelī Saṅgīta* cannot be narrowed down to any single tradition of music. In my conversation with Shyam Manohar Goswami, one of the most prominent scholar-practitioners of the Vallabha tradition, he stated a position similar to Pt Gokulotsavjī Mahārāja's. He points out the fact that a major portion of *Havelī Saṅgīta* compositions do not fit the *dhrupad-dhamār* format and are styled after some form of *prabandha* or regional music. Even the original composition of Nandadāsa's *rāsapañcādhyāyī* seems to be lost in the course of time as there is no clear opinion amongst the practitioners of *Havelī Saṅgīta* about it. While S.M. Goswami believes it to be some form medieval *prabandha* style, Pt Gokulotsavjī Mahārāja states its five chapters were perhaps rendered in five different *rāgas* to suit the mood of the characters in each act.

Especially noteworthy is the distinctive use of *ālāpacārī* or *ālāpa* in *Havelī Saṅgīta* that highlights the deep interweaving of the orthopraxis and music in *Puṣṭimārga*, which forms the next section of this introduction. While it serves as the opening section of musical rendition in Hindustani Classical, *dhrupad ālāpa* is typically an unmetered, unaccompanied, and improvised version of the *rāga* sung in a slow tempo to define its mood and notes. While these basic features are retained in *Havelī Saṅgīta, ālāpa* here is not just a prologue to the main melody but is also an ornamentation used in the middle of the song or sometimes as an entirely separate rendition of its own. *Ālāpa* thus serves two unique purposes in the process of devotional orthopraxis. Firstly, the ritual of waking up Kṛṣṇa at the break of the dawn is carried on tenderly to avoid an abrupt awakening. Hence, percussion instruments and cymbals are not used while the singing takes place at a slow tempo to a resemble a soft hum of a mother waking up her child. Unmetered and unaccompanied singing perfectly fits this finer emotive purpose and thus the early morning music is commonly rendered in *ālāpacārī* style. Secondly, *ālāpacārī* is used to welcome the mood of an upcoming festival or a shift in the season. Customarily, the *ālāpacārī* of *malhāra* and *basanta* are rendered before the monsoon and spring festivals respectively to highlight the change in the season and devotional mood. Considering the variety of such singing styles which are both improvised and at times indigenously developed within the tradition to suit its orthopraxis, it can be concluded that although *dhrupad-dhamār* constitutes the primary and most of its composition, *Havelī Saṅgīta* is a medley of several diverse singing styles.

Its music and poetry are integral fractions of both the orthopraxy and theology of *Puṣṭimārga*. Hence, it is crucial to note that the distinguishing characteristic of *Havelī Saṅgīta* is its liturgical value and the way it is used in the daily worship of Kṛṣṇa that precisely shapes its musical nuances. While it serves to enhance the devotional affectivities of both the worshipper and the worshipped, the words of its poetry depicting the theology of *Puṣṭimārga* are accepted as authoritative and sometimes indicative of the exegetical missing links in the tradition. I will illustrate both these aspects of *Havelī Saṅgīta* here, which paints a vivid picture of how music is employed in *Puṣṭimārga* as a soteriological tool in its orthopraxis as well as an exegetical summary of its theology.

## 2.4 Liturgical and Exegetical use of *Havelī Saṅgīta*

As stated earlier, *sevā*, which constitutes the core liturgy of the Vallabha Tradition, is as an intensely personal arrangement between the "Kṛṣṇa-for-worship" (*sevya-svarūpa*) and the devotee. It is a solid recreation of the life of Kṛṣṇa as a beloved cowherd in the present timeframe, while being equally mindful of his magnificent cosmic form. The practice of *sevā* is theologically rooted in the *Bhāgavata* and the cultural identity of Kṛṣṇa as a "dweller of Braja" (*brajavāsī*) and is consciously maintained at every stage of worship. This devotional engagement sets an intricate stage within the culture of Braja that acts as the background while the subjective affectivities of the devotee take the foreground. The process of daily worship thus interweaves the roles of both Yaśodā and the *gopikās*, as their unconditional love is an ideal of the highest form of devotion that one attempts to cultivate through the process of imitation and re-enactment. This development of devotion through "method acting" closely resembles the concept of *rāgānugā-bhakti* established by Rūpa Gosvāmī.[77] However, a crucial difference that sets the two apart is that while the *rāgānugā-bhakti* is a technique to act, live, and become the part one is playing, the idea of imitation in *Puṣṭimārga* is to retain one's personal identity. In other words,

77 David L. Haberman, *Acting as a Way of Salvation: A Study of Rāgānugā Bhakti Sādhanā* (New York: Oxford University Press, 2001), 65-80.

while Vallabha stresses on emulating the archetype of unconditional love of the *gopikās*, the particulars of their actions are not recommended, and thus, the devotee is ever mindful of the difference between their own identity and of the role they are playing. The idea here is to please Kṛṣṇa by recreating his divine plays as occurred in Braja, which means that devotees switch their role as and when the story changes. For instance, we find the festival of *Janamāṣṭamī* (the birth of Kṛṣṇa) is celebrated by emulating Yaśodā's parental love, while the festival of round dance (*rāsa-līlā*) emulates the love of the *gopikās*. Similarly, even in the process of daily worship the dominant mood changes as per the phase of the day. Following the life of Kṛṣṇa as per the *Bhāgavata*, we find that his mornings begin at the house of Nanda, while his time with the *gopikās* is often mentioned as occurring in the later part of his day. Re-enacting that order in *seva*, the devotee encapsulates the mood of Yaśodā at the daybreak and slowly shifts to the mood of the *gopikās* as the dusk approaches. This method of devotional worship highlights two crucial details that are relevant in the contextual framework of this work. Firstly, the concept of *seva* involves a complete engagement in the divine drama, where one actually "lives" with Kṛṣṇa rather than just worshipping him for a fixed amount of time. Secondly, it requires the mind to be solidly attuned to the divine plays of Kṛṣṇa and fully aware of his cosmic form to smoothly adopt the emotions of a parent, friend, and a beloved, amongst many others, all in one day.

While the theology of *Puṣṭimārga* views the pluralities of the world as an effect of the wilful playacting (*līlā*) of the supreme Lord, *sevā* is a process through which the devotee reciprocates this divine drama at an individual level. Remarkably similar to the manner music is used in a staged drama, even here it serves a two-fold purpose: firstly, it connects the devotee in the present space and time with Kṛṣṇa's era in Braja, and secondly, it acts as a subtle reminder of the shifts in the character and the dominant mood of the story throughout the process of worship. Thus, *Havelī Saṅgīta* is conscientiously rendered in a manner that its music never overrides its poetry, which brings us to the second aspect of this discussion. The poetry of these devotional compositions is considered to be infallible in the tradition, as it is regarded as an outflow of a perceived divine experience rather than a mere expression of devotion. For a clearer understanding of this aspect, it is crucial to know the story of its founders.

Most of what we know about *aṣṭa-chāpa*'s life and work comes from the *Vārtā* literature, a collection of hagiographical accounts of the ideal disciples of Vallabha and his son Viṭṭhalanātha. These stories, narrated

Gocāraṇa: Kṛṣṇa taking the cows out to graze.

*Vihāra:* Kṛṣṇa's pleasure sport with the gopikās in the forest.

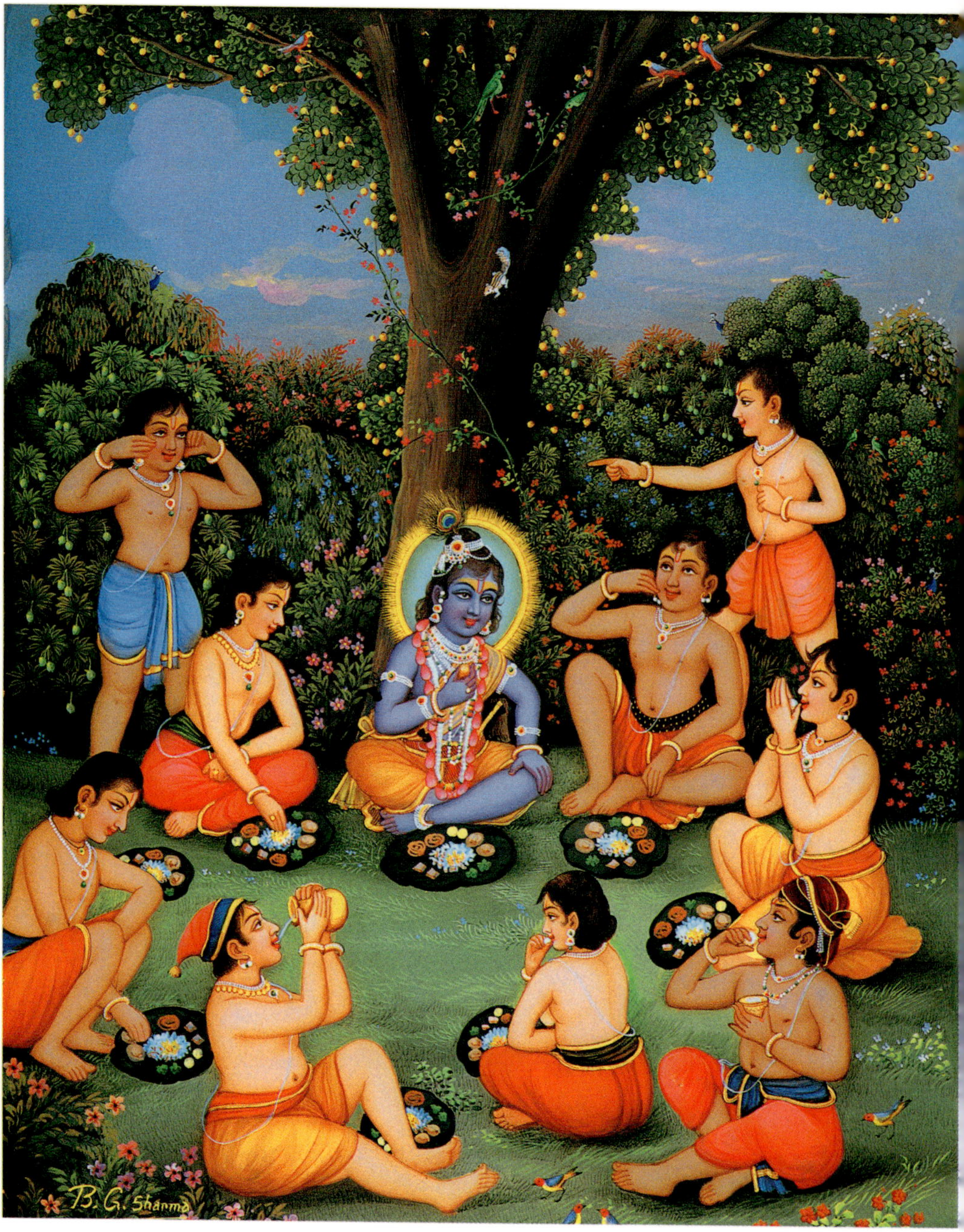


*Chāka:* Kṛṣṇa's meal in the forest with his cowherd friends.

Prathama-milana: The first meeting of Vallabhācārya with Śhrīnāthji atop the Govaradhana Mountain.

Beginning of Rāsa: Gopikās' arrival at the call of the flute.

रेवाशंकर शर्मा

Mahārāsa: The climactic dance of Kṛṣṇa with the Gopikās.

in *Braja-bhāṣa*, serve as a guidebook of devotion in this mundane age which is not the age of the descent (*anavatāra-kāla*) of the supreme Lord. In contrast, the *gopikās* provide an archetype of devotion, albeit in the wondrous "age of descent" (*avatāra-kāla*), where we find a direct and immediate contact with Kṛṣṇa. According to Vallabha, in the age of descent the conventional scriptural arrangements can be overturned by the grace of Lord (*prameya-bala*), and thus even extra-scriptural or condemnable methods are seen to lead the *gopikās* to the highest end. As stated earlier, this renders their devotional acts inimitable and exclusive in the current age, although the essence of their unconditional devotion continues to provide the basic framework and a model fit to follow. The stories from the *Vārtā* literature follow this exact template, where the disciples emulate the archetypical devotional model of the *gopikās* and at the same time follow the scriptural means (*pramāṇa-bala*) to achieve the same end. Hence, their life stories are considered to be the perfect guides of fructifying devotion in this ordinary age. We find that the author of the *Vārtā* literature thus proclaims them to be the ultimate fruit of all textual sources as the stories of these devotees are epitome of devotional perfection in the imperfect age of *Kali*.[78] Further, these eight poets, of which four are the disciples of Vallabha and four are of Viṭṭhalanātha, are mentioned in the *Vārtā* literature as the mortal incarnation of the eight primary *gopikās*, known as the *aṣṭa-sakhis*.[79] Although, the stories of these *aṣṭa-sakhīs* are not found in scriptural texts, they have a deep cultural root in the region of Braja and a crucial role to play in the liturgy of *Kṛṣṇa-bhakti* traditions, such as that of Caitanya and Vallabha. According to the *Vārtā* literature, these primary *gopikās* relived their divine play with Kṛṣṇa in the form of *aṣṭa-chāpa* when he took the form of Śrīnāthajī atop mount Govaradhana. As live commentaries on Kṛṣṇa's play, the poems of the *aṣṭa-chāpa* are valued in *Puṣṭimārga* as much as the testimony of the revealed scriptures or *śrutis*, despite the instances when their portrayal of the supreme Lord might seem against the scriptural version. At the same time, consistent with the fact that the *gopikās* are seen as the incarnations of the Vedic *śrutis* (*śrutirūpā*) rather than naïve cowherd girls,[80] even the *aṣṭa-chāpa*s are mentioned

78 *Caurasī Vaiṣṇavan Kī Vārtā*, edited by Balkishan Gabbad (Indore: Vaiṣṇava Mitra Maṇḍal, 2005) 1-2

79 Ibid, 428-429

80 Vallabhācārya, *Rāsapañcādhyāyī Śrī Subodhinī*, trans. Pandit J. Caturvedī (Varanasi: Chaukhambha Bharati Academy, 2017), 8.

as extraordinary devotees supremely graced with the knowledge of the Vedic texts. Some of their poems provide a readily intelligible version of Vallabha's exegeses, which suggests that their words strike a hermeneutical chord for the followers of the tradition. For instance, if we compare Hariram Vyas's *Braja-bhāṣā* rendition of the *rāsa* dance with that of Nandadāsa, we find the latter to be more consistent with the *Bhāgavata*'s version while the former is more of an intuitive work with liberties.[81] Furthermore, even at times when Nandadāsa sways from the parent model, a closer reading suggests that he is following Vallabha's commentary by rendering an elegant interpretation of its exegetical analysis rather than a literal translation of the original text. Thus, the poems of the *aṣṭa-chāpa* undeniably play a crucial hermeneutical role in the tradition, which is a rarely examined aspect in the study of *Havelī Saṅgīta*. I will explore this in greater detail later in this work through the annotations that will follow the translation of each chapter of the *rāsapañcadhyāyī*.

81 Guy L. Beck's "Two Braja Bhāṣā Versions of the Rāsa-Līlā Pancādhyāyī and Their Musical Performance in Vaiṣṇava Worship," *The Bhāgavata Purāṇa: Sacred Text and Living Tradition*, edited by Ravi M. Gupta and Kenneth R. Valpey (New York: Columbia University Press, 2013), 193.

THREE

# Nandadāsa: As a Devotee and a Poet

THE *VĀRTĀ* LITERATURE or *Vārtājī*, as it is respectfully known within the tradition, is a volume of hagiographical work categorised into two parts. Of these, the first part includes the stories of 84 disciples of Vallabha and the second part, which is divided into three volumes, narrates the stories of 252 disciples of Viṭṭhalanātha. The authorship is attributed to Gokulanātha (1552-1641 CE), the fourth son of Viṭṭhalanātha, who originally narrated these stories orally to his group of close, trusted disciples. During the time of Harirāya (1591-1716 CE), another celebrated classical commentator and poet of the Vallabha tradition, these stories were penned down alongside his constitutive commentary known as the *bhāva-prakāṣa*, which literally means "enlightening the devotional affectivities." Harirāya's commentary reveals the divine forms of the disciples, situating them in the eternal play of Kṛṣṇa (*nitya-līlā*), and also acts as a filler to connect the missing parts of the stories. But most significantly, it outlines the exegetical and liturgical motifs behind the turn of events that make the parent text more thorough. The *Vārtā* is almost never read without the *bhāva-prakāṣa*, making it an integral and indispensable part of the main text. Thus, I will use both these works to reconstruct the story of Nandadāsa here.[82] Divided into six anecdotal sketches (*prasaṅga*), the *Vārtā* reveals the remarkable journey of Nandadāsa from an amorous, sensual individual to a passionate poet and devotee. The story involves

82 *Do Sau Bāvan Vaiṣṇavan Kī Vārtā* – Vol. 3, edited by Balkishan Gabbad (Indore: Vaiṣṇava Mitra Maṇḍal, 2005), 293-320; henceforth, *Vārtā-3*.

numerous interactions with some historically famous figures such as Mughal emperor Akbar (1542-1605 CE) and his minister Birbal (1528-1586 CE), and more importantly, Saint Tulasīdās (1532-1623 CE), who is described as the older brother of Nandadāsa. Although the historicity of these anecdotes is disputed and not verifiable, they are unequivocally and uniformly accepted within the tradition and are crucial in shaping the characteristics of Nandadāsa at various stages of his devotional journey. Reconstructing all of the six episodes of his story goes beyond the scope of this work; hence, I will only focus on those aspects of his life that are directly relevant to the context of his poem.

Nandadāsa appears as the 241st disciple of Viṭṭhalanātha, in the third volume of the stories of the 252 disciples. The numerical order has little significance beyond the structural formatting of the text, for it is neither based on the chronological timeline of their initiation, nor does it imply any kind of devotional hierarchy. As stated earlier, the *aṣṭa-chāpas* are viewed as the incarnations of the eight primary *gopikās* (*aṣṭa-sakhī*), and in line with this narrative, Harirāya describes Candrarekhā to be the divine form of Nandadāsa.[83] As it is often the case, there is little to no information about the year or the date of Nandadāsa's birth nor any such biographical details. This is because, customarily, only the elements relevant to the devotional journey of the disciples are mentioned in the *Vārtā* literature.

In the very beginning of the story, Nandadāsa is introduced as the younger brother of Saint Tulsīdās, who initiates him in the *Rāmānandī* order of the devotional worship of Rāma. However, contrary to his more famous and highly pious brother, Nandadāsa is characterised as headstrong, salacious, and rather audacious. One day, very much against the wishes of Tulsīdās, who was apprehensive about allowing his brother to be on his own, Nandadāsa set out on a pilgrimage to Lord Raṇchoḍa, a form of Kṛṣṇa enshrined in Dwarka (Gujarat). Tulsīdās's fears come true when Nandadāsa strays away from his group and arrives in Siṁhanand, where he becomes smitten with the beautiful wife of a Kṣatriya[84] rather than Lord Raṇchoḍa. Enthralled by her elegance, he vows to not eat anything without seeing her once every day. As a few days pass, the Kṣatriya becomes deeply

83 *Do Sau Bāvan Vaiṣṇavan Kī Vārtā* – Vol. 3, edited by Balkishan Gabbad (Indore: Vaiṣṇava Mitra Maṇḍal, 2005), 293.

84 We are never told the name of this character, as he his only referred as *Kṣatriya* (warrior caste). It is common for the *Vārtā* to use the caste name or common nouns, such as a recluse (*virakta*), in place of the name.

embarrassed with this inappropriate routine of Nandadāsa, which had now become the talk of the town. As he was a disciple of Viṭṭhalanātha, the Kṣatriya decides to leave his town and settle in Gokul. However, when Nandadāsa hears of his departure, he follows the couple and they arrive on the banks of river Yamunā, which needed to be crossed to get to Gokul. In order to get rid of Nandadāsa, the Kṣatriya bribes the boatman to not take Nandadāsa across the river after he crosses over with his family. As he arrives at the residence of Viṭṭhalanātha, it is revealed to him that Nandadāsa is a divine soul (*daivī-jīva*) and everything that has happened was simply a medium to get Nandadāsa to Gokul. Viṭṭhalanātha then sends his men with a canoe to bring Nandadāsa to Gokul, and they find him singing songs of praise for Yamunā on her banks. The songs that Nandadāsa produced during this moment constitute a part of the 41 songs of praise for Yamunā (*iktālis-pada*), which are sung by adherents of the *Puṣṭimārga* in their daily worship. Although Yamunā is a Vedic goddess venerated across many Hindu traditions, her position in *Puṣṭimārga* is unparalleled. She is the most benevolent and revered goddess of tradition, who signifies unattributed, pure devotion (*nirguṇa-bhakti*) for Kṛṣṇa. She is also especially dear to him, for merely her affiliation instils unadulterated love for Kṛṣṇa (*śuddha-sneha*) in the individual souls and transforms their material passions into divine pursuits.[85] Evidently, Nandadāsa's devotional paeans express his instant and seemingly impossible transformation that comes about through his contact with Yamunā and eventually leads to his initiation in the tradition.[86] This inconceivable story of Nandadāsa's initiation outlines two contextually relevant themes of this text, namely, *puṣṭi* (grace) and *nirodha* (constraint). As stated earlier, through *puṣṭi* the individual soul overcomes the adversaries of time, space, and action, which is reflected in the way Nandadāsa gains control over his inappropriate act influenced by inauspicious time and space. Similarly, *nirodha* is a tool through which Kṛṣṇa steers or entices his devotees back to him from the worldly affairs, just like he did with the *gopikās*. Here, the text explains that Nandadāsa is brought to Gokul through a series of divine arrangements, signifying the inception of *nirodha*. When *nirodha*

85 See Vallabha's paean to Yamunā (*Yamunāṣṭakam*) in James D. Redington's *The Grace of Lord Krishna: The Sixteen Verse-Treatises (Ṣoḍaśagranthāḥ) of Vallabhacharya* (Delhi: Sri Satguru Publications, 2000), 8-9.

86 *Do Sau Bāvan Vaiṣṇavan Kī Vārtā* – Vol. 3, edited by Balkishan Gabbad (Indore: Vaiṣṇava Mitra Maṇḍal, 2005), 293-306.

is initiated, the individual soul is able to channelise the love that it has for its own self (*ahantā*), and worldly relationships as well as material possessions (*mamatā*), towards Kṛṣṇa. Especially the strong emotion of love directed towards the "significant other" in the material world is transformed into the unadulterated and unconditional form of love (*śudhha-prema*) for Kṛṣṇa as it happens with the *nirodha* of the *gopikās*. As Śuka, the narrator of the *Bhāgavata,* explains to his prime listener, Parīkṣit, the supreme Lord Kṛṣṇa is the repository of all emotions (*bhāvas*) and has the ability to transform even scripturally proscribed and negative emotions such as fear (*bhaya*) and resentment (*dveṣa*) into devotional states. Hence, it is not surprising that his supreme grace would transform ordinary love into the highest form of divine love (*Bhāgavata* 10.29.13-16). The process of initiation in the *Puṣṭimārga* symbolises the surrender of the former by devoting oneself in the service of Kṛṣṇa (*dāso'ham*) and of the latter by adopting a sense of utter belongingness to Kṛṣṇa (*kṛṣṇa-tavāsmi*). The process of *nirodha* is completed when this is internalised and Kṛṣṇa becomes the sole object of one's unwavering attention, which ultimately leads one to absolutely forget the material world, as it is exemplified in Nandadāsa's case. In other words, the *nirodha* of the *gopikās* is re-enacted in Nandadāsa's transformation, which establishes an archetype of devotion and *nirodha* in the ordinary age (*anavatāra-kāla*) juxtaposed against the age of descent (*avatāra-kāla*). This makes Nandadāsa's poetic rendition of the *rāsapañcādhyāyī* a highly personalised account of his own experience of *nirodha* in parallel to the *gopikās*.

Another significant anecdote is the one involving the exchange of letters between Tulsīdās and Nandadāsa after the latter's initiation, which brings forth a nuanced contrast between their respective expressions of devotion. I will present this war of words between two of the foremost devotees of Rāma and Kṛṣṇa by directly quoting the paraphrased version of their letters to each other.

Tulsīdās writes –

> *"You have discarded the virtue of fidelity in favour of adultery, which is not an appropriate code of conduct. When you come back to me, I will teach you to be faithful."*

To this, Nandadāsa responds –

> *"I was married to Rāma earlier, but Kṛṣṇa snatched me away and Rāma could*

> *not save me. Anyway, Rāma has vowed to only have one wife, so how will he handle another? He was unable to handle even one wife*[87] *while Kṛṣṇa graciously manages many women. So, I have now chosen Kṛṣṇa as my husband."*[88]

When read without any context, this exchange can come across as confusing, crude, and even sacrilegious. However, it has to be deciphered like a cypher, for each word here entails a delicate expression of devotion. Two ideas are immediately obvious. Firstly, devotion here is compared to a marriage. As very similar to a marital engagement where fidelity plays a fundamental role, in an act of devotion too, unwavering love focused on a single object of devotion (*niṣṭhā*) is the constitutional requirement. *Niṣṭhā* works akin to the one-pointed concentration of the yogic meditation (*dhyāna-dhāraṇa*), and hence, more than one object of devotion breaks the focal point in this spiritual marriage. Secondly, a devotee is analogous to a wife in this relationship as the femininity is used to demonstrate dependence in a conventional partnership. When a devotee is dependent on their Lord, it forms the pillar of *maryādā-bhakti* or duty-bound devotion that follows the conventions of the Vedic discipline. Tulsīdās and his lord Rāma, who is known to be *maryādā-puruśottama* or the lord of the Vedic discipline, together represent the duty-bound devotional partnership. From the perspective of Nāṭyaśāstra, duty-bound devotion can be best expressed in the mood of tranquillity (*śānta-rasa*) and humble servitude (*dāsa-bhāva*). In contrast, grace-bound devotion (*puṣṭi-bhakti*) is a radical reversal of this dynamic, for here, the supreme Lord becomes dependent on the devotee. This relationship involves a passionate ensemble of all moods as represented by Nandadāsa and Kṛṣṇa, who is described as the lord of the divine grace or *puṣṭi-puruśottama*. As stated earlier, the very definition of divine grace is the one that surpasses all Vedic conventions and Vallabha uses the *Bhāgavata* passage (9.4.66), in which Kṛṣṇa declares to be under the control of the *gopikās*, to describe the grace-bound devotion. It is a relationship in which the devotee is independent and the Lord acts according to the wish of his devotee.[89] This is another significant parallel between Nandadāsa and the *gopikās*, which further substantiates

87 This is a reference to Sītā's abduction in the *Rāmāyaṇa*.

88 *Do Sau Bāvan Vaiṣṇavan Kī Vārtā* – Vol. 3, edited by Balkishan Gabbad (Indore: Vaiṣṇava Mitra Maṇḍal, 2005), 308-309.

89 Vallabhācārya, *Bhāgavatārtha*, edited by Shyam M. Goswami (Kolhapur: Śrī Vallabha-vidyāpīṭha-Śrī Viṭṭhaleśaprabhucaraṇāśrma Trust, 1983) 354.

his expression of their grace-bound devotion through this poem. The *Vārtā* further states that Nandadāsa had originally produced a poetic composition of the entire 10th Canto. However, as this poetic version gained prominence it hampered the livelihood of the Brahmins of Braja, who were the professional orators of the *Bhāgavata*. On their request, Viṭṭhalanātha asked Nandadāsa to submerge his entire composition, except the one on the *rāsapañcādhyāyī*, into the Yamunā. Nandadāsa, thus, readily followed the behest of his guru and offered his devotional service to the river of love.[90]

The final passage of Nandadāsa's story outlines the abstruse and exotic nature of his compositions as they describe a higher order of devotion, which is comprehensible only to the one worthy of divine grace. It so happens that Tānsen, who was a disciple of Viṭṭhalanātha and also the royal musician of Emperor Akbar, once performed one of the compositions of Nandadāsa in the royal court. The final stanza of this composition describes the climax of the round-dance in following words:

> *"Rāsa mẽ Śrī Rādhe Śrī Rādhe muralī mẽ ehī raṭa,*
> *Nandadāsa gāve tahā̃ nipaṭa nikaṭa.*
>
> *The flute repeats the name of splendorous Rādhā in the round-dance, as Nandadāsa sings there sitting in proximity."*[91]

This description confuses the Emperor as he wonders how Nandadāsa could possibly view the round dance that happened in era of Lord Kṛṣṇa, and so, he summons him to elucidate the meaning behind his words. While Nandadāsa was divinely graced to experience the event of the *mahārāsa* described in the *Bhāgavata*, his devotion also allowed him to intimately participate in the everlasting divine play (*nitya-līlā*) that involves new *rāsa* that Kṛṣṇa has with his beloved devotees every day. This particular composition describes the latter as it describes the participation of Rādhā in the dance, who is mentioned neither in the *Bhāgavata* text nor in Nandadāsa's rendition of it. Rādhā is worshipped as the prime consort of Kṛṣṇa in the tradition, and her inclusion makes this a nuanced, experiential, and highly personal expression of devotion.

90 *Do Sau Bāvan Vaiṣṇavan Kī Vārtā* – Vol. 3, edited by Balkishan Gabbad (Indore: Vaiṣṇava Mitra Maṇḍal, 2005), 314.

91 Ibid., 317.

Unable to share this rare, esoteric essence of his words or override the Emperor's decree, Nandadāsa drops to the ground and leaves his mortal body.[92] Nandadāsa chose to give away his life rather than reveal his devotion to the world, which brings forth two significant ideas. Firstly, the emphasis given by Vallabha to keeping one's devotion private and secondly, it outlines the extent to which devotion is personalised in his tradition. This is a recurring theme in the *Vārtā* literature, where devotion is expressed as a highly private affair between the supreme Lord and his beloved devotee; the moment it is shared with the world, it loses its divinity. In describing this recondite nature of pure devotion, this passage also outlines the reverence that Nandadāsa's works command in the tradition of *Puṣṭimārga* and the delicate balance that its study demands. The scholarly pursuit needs to be arrayed with both the devotional expression of its composer and the impact it still has on his adherents today.

92 Ibid, 318-319.

# PART II

# Nandadāsa's Poetic Rendition of the *Rāsapañcādhyāyī*

ONE

# *Śuka-Stuti*: Paean to the Orator of the *Bhāgavata*

Verses 1–21

बंदन करूं कृपानिधान श्री शुक शुभकारी।।
शुद्ध जोतिमय रूप सदा सुंदर अविकारी।।१।।

*bandana karũ kṛpānidhāna śrī śuka śubhakārī,*
*śuddha jotimaya rūpa sadā sundara avikārī* (1)

I pay my obeisance to splendorous Śuka,
the auspicious repository of grace.
His form, consisting of pure light,
remains forever beautiful and unchanged.

हरि लीला रस मत्त मुदित नित विचरत जगमें।।
अद्‌त गति कहूं नहीं अटकव्हे निकसे मगमें।।२।।

*hari līlā rasa*[1] *matta mudita nita vicarata jagamẽ*
*adbhuta gati kahũ nahī̃ aṭakavhe nikase magamẽ* (2)

Intoxicated by the ecstasy of Hari's play,
he joyfully wanders the world.
Nothing obstructs his wondrous gait,
as he makes his way through the path.

1 *Rasa* has a varied range of meanings in dramaturgy as well as in the devotional aesthetics of Indian religious traditions. Especially in the context of Braja Vaiṣṇavism, *rasa* is used to denote inexplicable outpour of aesthetics sensuously savoured by the devotional emotivity of the worshipper (*bhakta*). To represent all these aspects as closely as possible and maintain the consistency, I am translating *rasa* as "ecstasy" all through this poem.

नीलोत्पल दल श्याम अंग नवयौवन भ्राजे।।
कुटिल अलक मुखकमल मानो अलि अवलि बिराजे।।३।।

*nīlotpala dala śyāma aṅga navayauvana bhrāje,*
*kuṭila alaka mukha-kamala māno ali avali birāje* (3)

His dark body radiates with blooming youth,
like a cluster of blue lotuses.
Curly locks sit on his lotus-face,
like a trail of swarming bees.

ललित भाल विशाल दिपति मानो निकर निशाकर।।
कृष्णभक्ति प्रतिबिंब तिमिरकूं कोटि दिवाकर।।४।।

*lalita bhāla viśāla dipati māno nikara niśākara,*
*kṛṣṇa-bhakti pratibiṁba*[2] *timirakū̃ koṭi divākara* (4)

His beautiful broad brows beam brightly,
like the abundance of many moons.
The reflection of his devotion for Kṛṣṇa
is like millions of suns
that casts away the darkness.

कृपा रंग रस एन नयन राजत रतनारे।।
कृष्ण रसासव पान अलस कछु घूम घुमारे।।५।।

*kṛpā raṅga rasa en nayana rājata ratanāre,*
*kṛṣṇa rasāsava pāna alasa kachu ghūma ghumāre* (5)

His eyes, the ecstatic store of graciousness,
are shot with the splendour of red.
Having sipped the spirituous ecstasy of Kṛṣṇa's eyes,
they seem somnolent and somewhat swirling.

श्रवण कृष्ण रस भवन गंड मंडल भल दरसें।।
परमानंद सों मिली सुमंद मुसकनि मधुबरसें।।६।।

2 In some versions, the word "*pratibandha*" is found instead of "*pratibiṁba*," which would change the meaning to "the obstacles in path of devotion to Kṛṣṇa." Here, the word "*timira*," which means darkness, would then be a metaphor for these obstacles.

*śravaṇa kṛṣṇa rasa bhavana gaṇḍa maṇḍala bhala darsẽ,*
*paramānanda sõ milī sumanda musakani madhu barasẽ* (6)

His ears, the ecstatic palace of Kṛṣṇa's stories,
make his curvy cheeks look pleasing.
Merging with the ultimate bliss,
his soft smile showers sweet nectar.

उन्नत नासा अधरबिंब शुक की छबि छीनी
तिन बिच अद्‌त भांत लसत कछु एक मसि भीनी।।७।।

*unnata nāsā adharabiṁba śuka kī chabi chīnī,*
*tina bica adbhuta bhā̃ta lasata kachu ek masi bhīnī* (7)

His curvy nose, and full red lips like a biṁba fruit,
steal away the glory of a parrot.
Between them in a wonderful way
sits a subtle sublime stroke of black.

कंबू कंठकी रेख देख हरि धर्म प्रकासें।।
काम को मद लोभ मोह जिहि निरखत नासें।।८।।

*kaṁbu kaṇṭha kī rekha dekha hari dharma prakāsẽ,*
*kāma krodha mada lobha moha jihin nirakhata nāsẽ* (8)

Oh, the spiral lines on his neck like those of a conch-shell
illumine the way to Hari.
A mere sight of it annihilates
lust, anger, pride, greed, and delusion.

उर वर पर अति छबि की भीर कछु बरणि न जाईं।।
जिहिं भीतर जगमगत निरंतर कुंवर कन्हाई।।९।।

*ura vara para ati chabi kī bhīra kachu baraṇi na jāī,*
*jihī̃ bhītara jagamagata nirantara kũvara kanhāī* (9)

Words fail to describe the glory
of the great grandeurs assembled on his chest.
For within it rests Lord Kṛṣṇa himself,
sparkling brightly forever.

सुंदर उदर उदार रोमावलि राजत भारी।।
हिये सरोवर रस भर चली मानो उमग पनारी।।१०।।

*sundara udara udāra romāvali rājata bhārī,*
*hiye sarovara rasa bhara chalī mano umaga panārī* (10)

Defined by a copious line of hair,
his broad torso gleams with glory.
His heart is a pool filled with ecstasy flowing forth,
much like a surging stream slowly springing out.

ता रस की कुंडका नाभी अस शोभित गहरी।।
त्रवली तामें ललित भांत जानो उपजत लहरी।।११।।

*tā rasa kī kuṇḍakā nābhī asa śobhita gaharī,*
*travalī tāmẽ lalita bhā̃ta jāno upajata laharī* (11)

That ecstatic stream sluices into a hollow deep,
and in his lustrous navel it seeps.
Emerging like little wavelets,
three delightful lines appear within.

अति सुदेश कटि देश सिंह सघन शोभित अस ।
युवजन मन आकर्षत बरसत सुधा रस ॥12॥

*ati sudeśa kaṭi deśa siṁha saghana śobhita asa,*
*yuvajana mana ākarașata barasata prema sudhā rasa* (12)

His elegant waist appears majestic,
like that of a lion in the wild.
Captivating the minds of the youth,
it showers the savorous elixir of love.[3]

गूढ जानु अजानु बाहु मद गज गति लोलें ।
गंगादिकन पवित्र करन अवनी में डोलें ॥13॥

*gūḍha jānu ajānu-bāhu mada gaja gati lolẽ,*
*gaṅgādikana pavitra karana avanī mẽ dolẽ* (13)

3 Here love means love for Kṛṣṇa – i.e., his mere appearance engulfs young minds with the love for Kṛṣṇa.

Having arms that reach his enigmatic knees,
he mirrors the gait of a euphoric tusker.
And when they swing as he walks in mighty strides,
he sanctifies the Ganges and other sacred sites!

सुंदर पद अरविंद मधुर मकरंद मुक्ति जहां।
मुनि मन मधुकर निकर सदा शोभित लोभी तहां ॥14॥

*sundara pada aravinda madhura makaranda mukti jahā̃,*
*muni mana madhukara nikara sadā śobhita lobhī tahā̃* (14)

Bearing the sweet nectar of salvation,
his lovely lotuslike feet look exquisite.
The minds of the saints surround them,
drawn like a swarm of insatiate bees.

जब दिनमणि श्रीकृष्ण द्दगनते दूर भये दुर ।
पसर पर्यो अँधियार सकल संसार घुमड घुर ॥15॥

*jaba dinamaṇi śrīkṛṣṇa dragana te dūra bhaye dura,*
*pasara paryo ãdhiyāra sakala saṁsāra ghumaḍa ghura* (15)

Like the jewel of dawn that fades over the sky,
so did Kṛṣṇa go far from the mortal eye.
The darkness then unfurled, falling all over
on the cyclical sublunary life on earth.

तिमिर ग्रसित सबलोक ओक देख दुखित दयाकर ।
प्रकट कियो अद्‌त प्रभाव श्रीभागवत विभाकर ॥16॥

*timira grasita saba loka oka dekha dukhita dayākara,*
*prakaṭa kiyo adbhuta prabhāva śrībhāgavata vibhākara* (16)

As the darkness devours all the realms, celestial and earthly,
the Merciful One was grieved by their plight.
And so he manifests a genesis wonderful and mighty,
splendorous *Bhāgavata*, the source, the light.

जे संसार अँधियार आगार में मग्न भए वर ।
तिन हित अद्‌त दीप प्रकट कीनो जु कृपाकर ॥17॥

*je saṁsāra ãdhiyāra āgāra mẽ magna bhaye vara,*
*tina hita adbhuta dīpa prakaṭa kīno ju kṛpā kara* (17)

They who wallow in the haven of darkness
and the ephemeral mortal worldliness.
This wonderful lamp is enkindled for their succour,
out of his gracious compassion.[4]

श्रीभागवत शुभ नाम परम अभिराम परम गति ।
निगम सार शकसार बिना गुरु कृपा अगम गति ॥18॥

*śrī-bhāgavata śubha nāma parama abhirāma parama gati,*
*nigama sāra śuka-sāra binā guru kṛpā agama gati* (18)

One with the auspicious name and highest taste,
the splendorous *Bhāgavata* bestows the highest state.
Bearing the gist of Śuka's words and essence of the Vedas,
it is unattainable without a guru's grace.

ताहि में पुनि अति रहस्य यह पंचाध्यायी ।
तन में जैसे पंचप्राण अस शुकमुनि गाई ॥19॥

*tāhi mẽ puni ati rahasya yaha pañcādhyāyī,*
*tana mẽ jaise pañca-prāṇa asa śuka-muni gāī* (19)

The most mysterious within the text
is this quintet, the cryptic of it all.
Like the five forces of life in the body,
Śuka the sage has rendered it so subtle and obscure.

परम रसिक एक मित्र मोहि तिन आज्ञा दीनी ।
ताहीतें यह कथा यथामति भाषा कीनी ॥20॥

*parama rasika eka mitra mohi tina ājñā dīnī,*
*tāhī te yaha kathā yathāmati bhāṣā kīnī* (20)

A connoisseur, an aesthete, and a friend of mine,
on his behest, I have commenced.

4 Here, "his" can indicate either Śrī Kṛṣṇa or Śrī Śuka, for the subject is not stated in the main verse.

And therefore, I construe this story
in my tongue, as per my wits, and as I fathom.

श्रीशुकमुनि रूप अनूप हें क्यों बरणे कवि नंद।
अब श्रीवृंदावन बरण हूं जहां श्रीवृंदावन चंद ॥21॥

*śrīśuka-muni rūpa anūpa hẽ kyõ baraṇe kavi nanda,*[5]
*aba śrīvṛndāvana baraṇa hũ jahā̃ śrī vṛndāvana canda* (21)

The splendorous sage Śuka, one with ineffable form,
how can this poet Nanda ever fully describe him?
And now, I portray the glorious Vṛndāvana,
wherein resides the lucent moon of Vṛndāvana![6]

5 In some versions, the latter part of this verse is found to be "*sõ baraṇe kavi nanda*," instead of "*kyõ baraṇe kavi nanda*," which would then translate to "thus described by poet Nanda."

6 The moon of Vṛndāvana is an oft-quoted metaphor for Śrī Kṛṣṇa.

TWO

# *Vṛndāvana-Varṇana*: Describing the Stage of the Divine Dance

Verses 22–54

अब सुंदर श्रीवृंदावन कों गाय सुनाउं ।
सकल सिद्धिदायक नायक पें सब निधि पाऊं ॥22॥

*aba sundara śrīvṛndāvana kõ gāya sunaũ,*
*sakala siddhidāyaka nāyaka pẽ saba nidhi pāũ* (22)

I now sing about and celebrate
the glories of beautiful Vṛndāvana.
I thereby discover the hero of this grove,
one who bestows all the fortunes of the world.

श्रीवृंदावन चिदघन कछू छबि बरनि न जाई ।
कृष्णललित लीला के काज धर रह्यो जडताई ॥23॥

*śrī-vṛndāvana cidaghana kachu chabi barani na jāī,*
*Kṛṣṇa lalita līlā ke kāja dhara rahyo jaḍatāī* (23)

Indescribable is the glory of the splendorous Vṛndāvana.
Its dense wilderness, with sentience thriving in its every essence.
But for the sake of Kṛṣṇa and his pleasing plays,
it changes its ways and becomes insentient.

जहां नग खग मृग लता कुंज वीरुध तृण जेते ।
नाहिन काल गुण प्रभाव सदा शोभित हे ते ते ॥24॥

*jahā̃ naga khaga mṛga latā kunja vīrudha tṛṇa jete,*
*nāhina kāla guṇa prabhāva sadā śobhita he tete* (24)

Where hills and mounts, birds and fowl,
flora, fauna, creepers, shrubs, and bowers.
Unaffected by time and its trait,
stay eternally ravishing forever.

सकल जंतु अविरुद्ध जहां हरि मृग संग चरहीं ।
काम क्रोध मद लोभ रहित लीला अनुसरहिं ॥25॥

*sakala jantu aviruddha jahā̃ hari mṛga saṅga carahī̃,*
*kāma krodha mada lobha rahita līlā anusarahī̃* (25)

Where all beings are unopposed to each other,
as Hari wanders with them and leads their way.
Bereft of desire and free from anger, without pride and greed,
blissfully they follow the divine play!

सब ऋतु संत वसंत लसत जहां दिनमणी शोभा ।
आन वनन जाकी विभूति कर शोभित शोभा ॥26॥

*saba ṛtu santa vasanta lasata jahā̃ dinamaṇi śobhā,*
*āna vanana jākī vibhūti kara śobhita śobhā* (26)

Where seasons stay in concert, and it is springtime forever,
the gem of dawn shines eternally, sprinkling its shimmer.
All other woods and groves are just its reflection,
mirroring its majesty and glittering with its glory.

ज्यों लक्ष्मी निजरूप अनूप चरण सेवित नित ।
भ्रूविलासतें जो विभूति जगमग रही जित तित ॥27॥

*jyõ lakṣmī nijarūpa anūpa caraṇa sevita nita,*
*bhrūvilāsatẽ jo vibhūti jagamaga rahī jita tita* (27)

Just as Lakṣmī in her uniquely essential form
perpetually serves the divine feet of Hari.
And the wealth of the world is merely her reflection,
shining at the gesture of her brow.

श्रीअनंत महिमा अनंत को बरण सके कवि ।
संकर्षण सों कछुक कही श्रीमुख जाकी छबि ॥28॥

*śrī ananta mahimā ananta ko baraṇa sake kavi,*
*sankarṣaṇa sõ kachuka kahī śrīmukha jākī chabi* (28)

Oh, its majestic magnificence, the one without an end,
this poet fails to describe it, because infinity cannot be penned.
Hari himself expresses it to Sankarṣaṇa,[7]
but only a smidgen, just a shade of its vision!

देवन में श्रीरमारमण नारायण प्रभु जस ।
वनन में श्रीवृंदावन सब दिन शोभित अस ॥29॥

*devana mẽ śrī-ramā-ramaṇa nārāyaṇa prabhu jasa,*
*vanana mẽ śrī-vṛndāvana saba dina śobhita asa* (29)

Just as Lord Nārāyaṇa stands foremost amongst the gods,
eternally delighting with splendorous Ramā,[8]
in his alluring abode.
So does the grand Vṛndāvana, foremost amongst the groves,
eternally glorious and delightful at all times.

या वन की वर बानिक या वनहीं वन बनि आवे ।
शेष महेश सुरेश गनेश हू पार न पावे ॥30॥

*yā vana kī vara bānika yā vanahī̃ bani āve,*
*śeṣa maheśa sureśa ganeśa hu pāra na pāve* (30)

The mystique of this beautiful grove has no simile,
standing as its own metaphor, unrivalled amongst the forests.
Unfathomable and beyond the ambit even for the gods,
be it be Śeṣa, Maheśa, Sureśa, or Gaṇeśa.[9]

---

7 The great serpent on whom Lord Viṣṇu rests, who is believed to hold the universe on his hood. As the foremost devotee of Viṣṇu, he always descends on earth alongside his Lord to serve him.

8 Goddess Lakṣmī.

9 Śeṣa is another name for Viṣṇu's serpent; Maheśa is another name for Śiva; Sureśa is a reference to Indra, the King of the Gods; and Gaṇeśa is the elephant-headed son of Śiva, who is known to be the remover of obstacles and worshipped before the beginning of any auspicious task.

जहां जेतिक द्रुम जात कल्पतरु सम सबलायक।
चिंतामणी सी भूमि सबे चिंतत फलदायक ॥31॥

*jahā̃ jetika druma jāta kalpataru sama sabalāyaka,*
*cintāmaṇī sī bhūmi sabe cintata phala-dāyaka* (31)

Where every creeper that grows and all its kind
match the radiance of the celestial Kalpataru.[10]
And this land, like the wish-fulfilling Cintāmaṇi,
grants all fruits that one desires.

तिन मधि एक कल्पतरू लग रही जगमग जोति ।
पत्र मूल फल फूल सकल हीरा मणि मोती ॥32॥

*tina madha eka kalpataru laga rahī jagamaga joti,*
*patra mūla phala phūla sakala hīrā maṇi motī* (32)

Amidst them stands a tree much like the Kalpataru itself,
that appears to glitter like a flickering flare.
The leaves, roots, and fruits, and blooms of the grove
appear like diamonds, jewels, and pearls of a treasure trove.

तिन मध्य तिनकी गंध लुब्ध अस गान करत अलि ।
वर किन्नर गंधर्व अप्सरा तिन पर गई बलि ॥33॥

*tina madha tinakī gandha lubdha asa gāna karata ali,*
*vara kinnara gandharva apsarā tina para gaī bali* (33)

Amidst them, covetous for its nectar and lured by its fragrance,
rendering a melodic song, the bees swarm, buzz, and hum.
Celestial symphonists, songsters, and nymphs
surrender their skills on hearing the song of Vṛndāvana's bees!

अमृत फुहि सुख गुही अति सुही परत रहत नित ।
रास रसिक सुंदर पिय के श्रम दूर करन हित ॥34॥

10 Very much like the wish-fulfilling gem Cintāmaṇi, Kalpataru too is a celestial wish-fulfilling tree believed to be in Indra's garden.

*amṛta phuhi sukha guhī ati suhī parata rahata nita,*
*rāsa rasika sundara piya ke śrama dūra karana hita* (34)

Ambrosia sprouts while pleasure entwines,
and a stream of nectar exudes forever here.
Just for the sake of easing the fatigue
of the beautiful beloved, the savant of the round dance.

ता सुरतरु में अवर एक अद्‌त छबि छाजे ।
शाखा दल फल फूलन हरि प्रतिबिंब बिराजे ॥35॥

*tā surataru mẽ avara eka adbhuta chabi chāje,*
*śākha dala phala phūlana hari pratibiṁba birāje* (35)

In the divine tree, which is one of its kind,
a wonderful image invariably shines.
In its trunk, branches, fruits, and flowers,
a reflection of Hari forever resides.

ता तर कोमल कनक भूमि मणिमय मोहित मन ।
देखियत सब प्रतिबिंब मानो धर में दूसरो वन ॥36॥

*tā tara komala kanaka bhūmi maṇimaya mohita mana,*
*dekhiyata saba pratibimba māno dhara mẽ dūsro vana* (36)

Underneath the tree lies the land that beguiles the heart,
bejewelled and made of gold, yet gentle and soft.
A mirror-image it creates thereof
as if another grove lies beneath the grove above.

थलज जलज झलमलत ललित बहु भ्रमर उडावे ।
उड उड परत पराग कछु छबि कहत न आवे ॥37॥

*thalaja jalaja jhalamalata lalita bahu bhramara uḍāve,*
*uḍa uḍa parata parāga kachu chabi kahata na āve* (37)

The blooms born in land and the blooms born in water
wave with poise as the swarm of bees, buzz, and rejoice.

When they fly, flit and flutter with sprinkling the pollen around, their beauty cannot be expressed in words.

श्रीयमुनाजी प्रेम भरीं नित बहत सु गहरी।
मणि मंडित बहु भांत दूर होय परसत लहरी ॥38॥

*śrī-yamunājī prema bharī̃ nita bahata su gaharī,*
*maṇi manḍita bahu bhā̃ta dūra hoya parsata laharī* (38)

Splendorous Yamunā, the love-filled river flowing forever,
deep-down drifts its water and deep-down drifts its love.
Sands and shore, adorned with jewels of every kind,
and its delightful waves spread far and wide.

तहां एक मणिमय वितस्त को संकु सुभग अति ।
तापर षोडश दल सरोज अद्त चक्राकृति ॥39॥

*tahā̃ eka maṇimaya vitasta ko sanku subhaga ati,*
*tāpara ṣodaśa dala saroja adbhuta cakrākṛti* (39)

There sprawls an ornate island,
within which lies an auspicious conch.
On it rests a lovely sixteen-petaled lotus,
bearing a wonderful annular shape.

मध्य कमनीय करणिका सब सुख सुंदर कंदर ।
तहां राजत व्रजराज कुंवर वर रसिक पुरंदर ॥40॥

*madhya kamanīya karaṇikā saba sukha sundara kandara,*
*tahā̃ rājata vraja-rāja kũvara vara rasika purandara* (40)

Amidst that lotus, a desirous pericarp divine
seems a haven of delight, like a pleasing ravine.
There he manifests, the King of Vraja, like the King of Gods,
the aesthete, the connoisseur, the ecstatic Lord.

निकर विभाकर द्ति मेटत शुभकौस्तुभ मणि अस ।
सुंदर नंदकुंवर उर लागत रुचिर उडु जस ॥41॥

*nikara vibhākara dyuti meṭata śubha-kaustubha maṇi asa,*
*sundara nandakũvara ura lāgata rucira uḍu jasa* (41)

One that fades a multitude of moons and their light,
the auspicious Kaustubha gleams so bright.[11]
And yet, a sheer shimmer of the stars it seems,
when the beautiful son of Nanda dons it on his chest.

मोहन अद्‌त रूप कहत न आवे छबि ताकी।
अखिल अंड व्यापी जु ब्रह्म आभा हे जाकी ॥42॥

*mohana adbhuta rūpa kahata na āve chabi tākī,*
*akhila aṇḍa vyāpī ju brahma ābhā he jākī* (42)

Wonderful is the form of Mohana,[12]
can anyone describe it fully?
For his divine radiance, the splendour of Brahman
pervades the entire cosmic egg.

परमात्मा परब्रह्म सबनके अंतरयामी ।
नारायण भगवान धर्मकर सबके स्वामी ॥43॥

*parmātma parabrahma sabana ke antarayāmī,*
*nārāyaṇa bhagavāna dharmakara sabake svāmī* (43)

He is the Supreme Self, the Absolute Being,
and the inner guide of every being.
O Lord Nārāyaṇa! The master of all,
and the bearer of the eternal cosmic law.

बाल कुमार पौगंड धर्म आक्रांत ललित तन ।
धर्मी नित्य किशोर कान्ह मोहत सबको मन ॥44॥

*bāla kumāra paugaṇḍa dharma ākrānta lalita tana,*
*dharmī nitya kiśora kānhā mohata saba ko mana* (44)

From infancy to childhood to boyhood he goes;
pleasing at every age, he lets nature take its course.

11 A divine jewel that Lord Viṣṇu wears on his chest.

12 Another name for Kṛṣṇa.

Charming Kānhā,[13] the bearer of cosmic order,
entices every heart as he stays youthful forever.

कंठ मुक्तन की माल ललित वनमाल धरें पिय ।
मंद मधुर हस पीतवसन फरकत करखत हिय ॥45॥

*kanṭha muktana kī māla lalita vanamālā dharẽ piya,*
*manda madhura hasa pīta vasana pharakata karakhata hiye* (45)

The beloved Lord wears a necklet of pearls around his neck,
and is adorned by a grand garland of wildflowers.
A sweet soft smile he bears and a yellow garment he wears,
which flips and flaps, fluttering the hearts around.

अस अद्‌त गोपाल बाल सबकाल वसत जहां ।
याही ते वैकुंठ वैभव कुंठित लागत तहां ॥46॥

*asa adbhuta gopāla bāla sabakāla vasata jahā̃,*
*yāhīte vaikunṭha vaibhava kunṭhita lāgata tahā̃* (46)

Where dwells this wonderful boy, the keeper of cows,
there dwell all the seasons and the time itself.
And hence even the glory of Vaikunṭha,
the abode of the supreme Lord,
pales at the sight of this divine grove.

यद्यपि सहज माधुरी विपिन सब दिन सुखदाई ।
तदपि रंगीली शरद समय मिल अति छबि पाई ॥47॥

*yadyapi sahaja mādhurī vipina saba dina sukhadāī,*
*tadapi raṅgīlī śarada samaya mila ati chabi pāī* (47)

This naturally pleasing grove
is although eternally delightful,

13 Kānhā, which is short for Kanhaiyā, is a Braja alteration for the name Kṛṣṇa, and is often used with love and adoration. As the main verse contains both names of Kṛṣṇa, namely, Kānhā and Mohana, I do not think they are used equally as proper nouns here. As *mohana* also means "charmer," hence, it is more appropriate to see it as an adjective, which poetically highlights the idea that charmer is charmed by the charm of the Braja women.

Yet indeed, when the time of autumn arrives,
merging with the colours of the fall, it looks simply exquisite.

ज्यों अमोल नग जगमगाय सुंदर जराय संग ।
रूपवंत गुणवंत बहुर भूषण भूषित अंग ॥48॥

*jyõ amola naga jagamagāya sundara jarāya saṅga,*
*rūpavanta guṇavanta bahura bhūṣaṇa bhūṣita aṅga* (48)

Just like a priceless precious jewel shining beautifully,
but when studded with other gems, it glitters more than ever.
And just like a beautiful and virtuous person,
although naturally alluring,
when adorned elegantly, looks more ravishing than ever.

रजनी मुख सुख देत ललित प्रफुल्लित जु मालती।
जो नवयौवन पाये लसत गुणवती बालती ॥49॥

*rajanī mukha sukha deta lalita praphullita ju mālatī,*
*jo nava-yauvana pāye lasata guṇavatī bālatī* (49)

The face of moon like a boon, sheer joy it showers,
it makes the lovely Mālati bloom, along with other flowers.
As if a noble maiden has been blessed with youthful glow,
Seems all the more stunning than ever.

छबि सों फूले फूल अवर अस लगी लुनाई ।
मानो शरद की क्षपा छबीली विहसत आई ॥50॥

*chabi sõ phūle phūla avara asa lagī lunāī,*
*māno śarada kī kṣapā chabīlī vihasata āī* (50)

The florets flower with magnificence,
like a lovely spread of crops waving along.
Seems like a beautiful night of autumn
that walks with simper and ambles with smile.

ताही समय उडुराज उदित रस रास सहायक ।
कुंकुम मंडित प्रिया वदन जानो नागरि नायक ॥51॥

*tāhī samaya uḍu-rāja udita rasa rāsa sahāyaka,*
*kuṅkuma-maṇḍita priyā vadana jāno nāgari nāyaka* (51)

And then the king of the stars rises with a scarlet hue,
behoving the ecstatic round dance.[14]
As if a belle unveiled her blushed crimson face,
at the sight of her beloved hero.

कोमल किरण अरुण वन में व्यापि रही यों ।
मनसिज खेल्यो फाग घुमड घुररह्यो गुलाल ज्यों ॥52॥

*komala kiraṇa aruṇa vana mẽ vyāpī rahī yõ,*
*manasija khelyo phāga ghumaḍa ghura rahyo gulāla jyõ* (52)

Soft scarlet sheen spreads across the night,
as the moon swaddles the grove with its lovely light.
The god of love plays Holī, or so it appears,
as if a thick mist of gulāla[15] swathes all in its sphere.

फटक छटासी किरण कुंज रंध्रन जब आई ।
मानो वितनु वितान सुदेश बनाय तनाई ॥53॥

*phaṭaka chaṭāsī kiraṇa kunja randhrana jaba āī,*
*māno vitanu vitāna sudeśa banāya tanāī* (53)

Shafts of the moonlight, like that of a quartz crystal
are filtered through the lush alcove.
And a silver canopy it forms atop this lustrous land,
as if the god of love designed it with his own hand!

मंदमंद चल चारु चंद्रमा अति छबि पाई ।
उझकत है मानो रमा रमण पिय कौतुक आई ॥54॥

*manda-manda cala cāru candramā ati chabi pāī,*
*ujhakata he māno ramā ramaṇa piya kautuka āī* (54)

---

14 King of the stars (*uḍu-rāja*) is a common reference for the "moon" in Braja Bhāṣā poetics.

15 A traditional name for the colours with which Holī is played, especially referring to the colour red.

The majestic moon is poised with flair,
as it moves softly sauntering mid-air.
As if Ramā, the abode of lord's delight, arrives frolicking,
beckoned by her beloved and curious for his play.

इति रासक्रीडा वर्णने वृन्दावन वर्णनः

|| *iti rāsakrīḍā varṇane vṛndāvana varṇanaḥ* ||

So ends the portrayal of Vṛndāvana in the description of *rāsa*.

THREE

# Chapter I: The Beginning of *Rāsalīlā* and the Call of the Flute

Verses 55–133

तब लीनी करकमल योगमाया सी मुरली ।
अघटित घटना चतुर बहुर अधरामृत जुरली ॥55॥

*taba līnī kara-kamala yoga-māyā sī muralī,*
*aghaṭita ghaṭanā catura bahura adharāmṛta juralī* (55)

And then he takes the alluring flute in his lotus-like hands,
like the enthralling yogic force of Lord,
it reveals the route for the *rāsa* land.
And unique occurrence then commences,
with the clever call of flute, as the nectar of his lip merges!

जाकी ध्वनि ते अगम निगम प्रकटे बडनागर ।
नादब्रह्म की जननी मोहनी सब सुखसागर ॥56॥

*jākī dhvani te agama nigama prakaṭe baḍanāgara,*
*nāda-brahma kī jananī mohanī saba sukha-sāgara* (56)

The call of flute is the root
of the primal Vedic word;
it begets the Agama and the Nigama,[16]
and every wisdom ever heard.

16 Nigama is another name for the Vedas while Agama (Āgama in Sanskrit) refers to a large body of canonical texts found primarily in Sanskrit, Tamil, and Telegu languages.

The mother of the primordial sound of creation,
alluring as ever and an ocean of elation!

पुन मोहन सों मिलि कछुक कल गान कियो अस ।
वामविलोचन बाल तिनके मन हरण होय जस ॥57॥

*puna mohana sõ mili kachuka kala gāna kiyo asa,*
*vāma-vilocana bāla tinake mana haraṇa hoya jasa* (57)

It unites with Mohana to top it all,
rendering such a tender but esoteric song.
The beautiful belles with angled gaze
have their hearts taken stolen by its maze.

मोहन मुरली नाद श्रवण सुन्यो सब किनहीं।
यथा जथा विधिरूप तथाविधि परस्ये तिनहीं ॥58॥

*mohana muralī nāda śravaṇa sunyo saba kinahī̃,*
*yathā jathā vidhirūpa tathā vidhi parasye tinahī̃* (58)

The sound of Mohana's flute
is heard by one and all.
However, few are ordained to receive its message,
as served by their destiny and as per the form of their fate.

तरणि किरण ज्यों मणि पषान सबहिन कों परसे ।
सूरजकांत मणि विना नहिं कहू पावक दरसे ॥59॥

*taraṇi kiraṇa jyõ maṇi paṣāna sabahina kõ parase,*
*sūraja-kānta maṇi vinā nahī̃ kahū pāvaka darase* (59)

Just as every stone and every jewel in the mine
is touched equally by the rays of sunshine,
and yet besides the crystal quartz, the friend of the sun,
no other stone reflects its rays as bright as a glaring flare.

सुनत चली ब्रजबधू गीत ध्वनि को मारग गहि।
भवन भीत द्रुम कुंज पुंज कितहु अटकी नहिं ॥60॥

*sunata calī braja-badhū gīta dhvani ko māraga gahi,*
*bhavana bhīta druma kunja punja kitahū aṭakī nahī̃* (60)

The Braja women set forth hearing the flute,
on the road paved by its melodic tune.
Nothing stops their stride, when the sound of the flute calls,
not the group of woods and trees, nor their house and its walls.

नादामृत को पंथ रंगीलो सूक्ष्म भारी ।
तिहि व्रजतिय मग चली आन कोऊ नहिं अधिकारी ॥61॥

*nādāmṛta ko pantha raṅgīlo sūkṣma bhārī,*
*tihi brajatiya maga calī āna koū nahī̃ adhikārī* (61)

Nectar of seraphic sound waves paved the colourful course,
radiant but subtle and as abstruse as its source.
No one else is thus allowed to tread on the path
on which the lovely Braja women walk.

शुद्ध प्रेममय रूप पंचभूतन तें न्यारी।
तिने कहा कोऊ गहे जोति सी जग उजियारी ॥62॥

*śuddha prema-maya rūpa pañcabhūtana te nyārī,*
*tine kahā koū gahe joti sī jaga ujiyārī* (62)

Pure love defines their form,
distinct from the five elements.
Like a raging fire they appear,
who can ever contain them?

जो रुक गई घर अति अधीर गुणमय शरीर वस ।
पुन्य पाप प्रारब्ध सच्यो तन नाहिन पच्यो रस ॥63॥

*jo ruka gayī ghara ati adhīra guṇa-maya śarīra vasa,*
*punya pāpa prārabdha sacyo tana nāhina pacyo rasa* (63)

And then barred by the attributes of their mortal body,
they who stop in their house are lonely and restless.

Due to the all merits and demerits amassed,
they fail to absorb the ecstasy in its divine pureness.

परम दुसह श्रीकृष्ण विरह दुःख व्याप्यो तिनमें ।
कोटि वरस लग नर्क भोग अघ भूक्ते छिनमें ॥64॥

*parama dusaha śrī-kṛṣṇa viraha duḥkha vyāpyo tinamẽ,*
*koṭi varasa laga narka bhoga agha bhukte chinamẽ* (64)

Intolerable are pangs of separation from Kṛṣṇa,
as the sorrow slowly permeates them.
Millions of years of hellfire are suffered through the fire within,
and in a flash, it burns away their flaws, faults, and sins.

पुन रंचक धर ध्यान पियहि पररंभ दियो जब ।
कोटि स्वर्ग सुख भुक्ते क्षीण मंगल कीने सब ॥65॥

*puna rañcaka dhara dhyāna piyahi pararaṁbha diyo jaba,*
*koṭi svarga sukha bhukte kṣīṇa maṅgala kīne saba* (65)

They briefly meditate on their beloved,
embracing him in that moment.
They experience millions of years of the pleasure of paradise,
and are thus rendered auspicious in that fleeting moment.

धातु पात्र पाखान परस कंचन व्हे सोहें ।
नंदसुवन सों परम प्रेम यह अचरज कोहें ॥66॥

*dhātu pātra pākhāna parasa kañcana vhe sohẽ,*
*nanda-suvana sõ parama prema yaha acaraja kohẽ* (66)

The alchemy of the philosopher's stone
turns any metal to radiant gold.
Why does it then astound that unconditional and pure love
for the son of Nanda,
makes them sacred as well?

ते पुन तिहिं मग चली रंगीली त्यज गृह संगम ।
मानो पिंजरन ते घुटे छुटे नव प्रेम विहंगम ॥67॥

*te puna tihĩ maga calī raṅgīlī tyaja gṛha saṅgama,*
*māno piñjarana te ghuṭe chuṭe nava prema vihaṅgama* (67)

And so they take a colourful lane,
as they forsake their homes and its bonds.
Like a bird in a cage stifled all its age
is freed to attain a sky full of new love.

केतिक तरुणी गुणमय शरीर तिहिं सहित चली दुक ।
मात पिता पति बंधु रहे झुक नाहिन रही रुक ॥68॥

*ketika taruṇī guṇa-maya śarīra tihĩ sahita calī duka,*
*māta pitā pati bandhu rahe jhuka nāhina rahī ruka* (68)

Some youthful women with their mortal bodies
make their way towards the blissful call.
Mother, father, husband, and brothers,
even friends stop their way,
but to none they yield,
so resolutely they do proceed.

श्रावण सरिता रुके नहीं करे कोटि यत्न अति ।
कृष्ण हरे जाके मन ते क्यों रुके अगम अति ॥69॥

*śrāvaṇa saritā ruke nahĩ kare koṭi yatna ati,*
*kṛṣṇa hare jāke mana te kyõ ruke agama gati* (69)

Just like a brook under the Śrāvaṇa moon,
that is unstoppable by any force,
and runs relentless at the onset of monsoon.
And so do they who lose their hearts
to Kṛṣṇa's alluring arts.
Unattainable becomes their pace.
Why would they stop ever their race?

चलत अधिक छबि फ़बित श्रवण मणिकुडल झलकें ।
संकित लोचन चपल चारु मानो बिलुलित अलकें ॥70॥

*calata adhika chabi fabita śravaṇa maṇi-kuṇḍala jhalakẽ,*
*saṅkita locana capala cāru māno bilulita alakẽ* (70)

Pleasant they look with their hurried pace,
and the bejewelled earrings swaying grandly
adds to their naturally exotic grace.
Playful eyes and glance askance
thus enhance their flair,
and their lovely locks sway amok
with their blowing hair.

यद्यपि कहूं के कहूं वधून आभरण बनाये ।
हरि पिय पें अनुसरत जहां के तहां चल आये ॥71॥

*yadyapi kahũ̃ ke kahũ̃ vadhūna ābharaṇa banāye,*
*hari piya pẽ anusarata jahā̃ ke tahā̃ cala āye* (71)

Their grand and abundant jewellery,
although made with great gusto,
in hasty passion they've fully forgone.
As they follow their beloved Hari's song,
the adornments are all brushed aside
as they rush to be by his side!

कहुं देखियत कहुं नाहिन वधू वन बीच यों ।
विजुरण की सी पांति सघनवन मांझ चलत यों ॥72॥

*kahũ dekhiyata kahũ nāhina vadhū vana bīca banī yõ,*
*vijuraṇa kī sī pā̃ta saghana vana mā̃jha calata yõ* (72)

As they make their way amidst the woody terrene,
sometimes they are surely seen,
and at times they go quite unseen.
Walking through the deep woods,
like a thunderbolt from the blue,
they appear like a sparkling queue.

आय उमग सों मिली रंगीली गोप वधू अस ।
नंदसुवन सुंदर सागर सों प्रेमनदी जस ॥73॥

*āye umaga sõ milī raṅgīlī gopa vadhū asa,*
*nandasuvana sundara sāgara sõ prema-nadī jasa* (73)

The flamboyant cowherd women,
are lavish with splendour
when they arrive with great passion,
vibrant, vivid, and full of colour!
They come streaming to him,
just like a river replete with love,
and meet the son of Nanda,
the divine ocean of beauty.

परम भागवत रत्न रसिकजु परीक्षित राजा ।
प्रश्न कीयो रस पुष्टि करन निज सुख के काजा ॥74॥

*parama bhāgavata ratna rasīkaju parīkṣita rājā,*
*praṣṇa kīyo rasa puṣṭi karana nija sukha ke kājā* (74)

The connoisseur of all ecstasy,
and the listener of the first order,
king Parīkṣita, is the jewel
among the Bhāgavata hearers.
He then poses a question,
solely with the intention
to nourish the divine ecstasy
and enhance his blessed joy.

श्रीभागवत को पात्र जान जग के हितकारी ।
उदर दरी में करी कान्ह जाकी रखवारी ॥75॥

*śrī bhāgavata ko pātra jāna jaga ke hitakārī,*
*udardarī mẽ karī kānha jākī rakhavārī* (75)

As the worthy hearer of the splendorous Bhāgavata,
and for the welfare of the world,
He was sheltered by Kānhā from an outright doom,
and protected by the supreme Lord in his mother's womb![17]

17 This is a reference to the story of Parīkṣit's birth found in the *Bhāgavata* (1.8.9). It is stated that Aświtthāmā, the son of Droṇa, who the guru of the Kuru princes, directed a deadliest divine weapon known as Brahmāstra towards Parīkṣit when he was in his mother Uttarā's womb to destroy the lineage of the Pāṇḍavas. Although Brahmāstra hit its target, Kṛṣṇa intervened and brought Parīkṣit back to life. Nandadāsa is saying here that Kṛṣṇa did that because he knew that Parīkṣit would be foremost of the devotees and would be the reason

जाकों सुंदरश्याम कथा छिन छिन नई लागे ।
ज्यो लंपट पर युवती बात सुन सुन अनुरागे ॥76॥

*jākõ sundara-śyāma kathā china china naī lāge,*
*jyõ lampaṭa para yuvatī bāta suna suna anurāge* (76)

When the stories of beautiful Śyāma[18] are told anew,
every moment for him seems gratifying and new.
Just like a dissolute man who is elated with amour,
as he hears the pleasing tales of a young paramour.

अहो मुनि क्यों गुणमय शरीर सों पाये हें हरि ।
जान भजे कमनीय कांत नहीं ब्रह्मभाव करि ॥77॥

*aho munī kyõ guṇa-maya śarīra sõ paye hẽ hari,*
*jāna bhaje kamanīya kānta nahī̃ brahma-bhāva kari* (77)

How do they engage with Hari, O Sage,
and why do they attain him with their worldly bodies?
They adore him like their beloved,
going against the Vedic norm.
They do not worship him as absolute Brahman,
despite knowing his cosmic form.

तब कह्यो श्रीशुकदेव अहो यह अचरज नाहीं ।
सर्व भाव भगवान कान्त जिनके हियमाहीं ॥78॥

*taba kahyo śrī-śukadeva aho yaha acaraja nāhī̃,*
*sarva bhāva bhagavāna kānta jinake hiya māhī̃* (78)

Splendorous Śukadeva then replies,
O king, this is no surprise!
The supreme God is the bearer of all moods,
whether sensual, mundane, or divine.
And so, he rests in their heart,
honouring love of all kinds!

---

that the divine fruit of the *Bhāgavata* would be retold and made available to common human beings.

18 Another name for Kṛṣṇa, literally meaning "the black one." In the later verses I often translate this as "the dark Lord" to bring out the devotional emotivity and aesthetics of the poetry.

परम दुष्ट शिशुपाल बालपन तें निंदक अति ।
जोगिन जो गति दुर्लभ सुलभ पाई है सो गति ॥79॥

*parama duṣṭa śiśupāla bālapana tẽ nindaka ati,*
*jogina jo gati durlabha sulabha pāī hai so gati* (79)

Look at the sinful and sinister Śiśupāla,
who was the denigrator of all things good
since his very childhood.
And yet he attained with ease
an exceptionally rare fate,
that which even the yogis crave,
the ultimate salvation great.[19]

यही रस ओपी गोपी सब त्रियन तें न्यारी ।
श्रीकमलनयन गोविंदचंद की प्राण सू प्यारी ॥80॥

*yahi rasa opī gopī saba triyana te nyārī,*
*śrī-kamala-nayana govinda-canda kī prāṇa su pyārī* (80)

Suffused with this salvific ecstasy
are these cowherd women,
And so they are distinct and unique
amongst all other maidens.
The moon of the cowherd folks,
and the one with lotus eyes,
the splendorous Govinda adores them,
dearer than his life.

तिनके नूपुर नाद सुने जब परम सुहाये ।
तब हरि के मन नयन सिमिट सब श्रवनन आये ॥81॥

*tina ke nūpur nāda sune jaba parama suhāye,*
*taba hari ke mana nayana simita saba śravaṇana āye* (81)

19 According to the Purānic myths, Śisupāla was a great devotee and one of the two doormen of the gates of Vaikunṭha, the eternal abode of Viṣṇu. He was cursed to fall from grace; however, Lord Viṣṇu redeemed him despite all his denigrations. Śuka is making this reference to argue that if Lord even redeems the ones who denigrate him then why would he not honour the genuine love of his dearest *gopikās*?

Tuneful anklet bells he hears chiming at a distance;
sounds of tiny bells please his divine self.
To hear that lovely sound,
Hari's eyes and mind then come together
with his divine ears.

रुनक झुनक पुन छबीली भांत सब प्रकट भई जब ।
पिय के अंग अंग सिमिट मिले हें छबीले नयन जब ॥82॥

*runaka jhunake puna chabīlī bhānta saba prakaṭa bhayī jaba,*
*piya ke aṅga aṅga simiṭa mile hẽ chabīle nayana taba* (82)

The charming sound of jingle jangle
soon fills the ambience.
Trinkets tinkle together,
at their lovely presence.
Every part of their beloved's form,
they intently gaze and stare,
and their lovely eyes are locked on him,
enhancing their flair.

कुंजन कुंजन निकसत शोभित वर आनन अस ।
तम के कोन मध्य तें निकर राका मयंक जस ॥83॥

*kuñjana kuñjana nikasata śobhita vara ānana asa,*
*tama ke kona madhya te nikara rākā mayaṅka jasa* (83)

Then they surface, with their faces
beaming like moonshine.
Emerging out of many groves,
they appear splendorously fine.
As if rises many full moons,
from within the dark black grove.
And the radiance of many moons,
it appears like a lucent trove.

सबके मुख अवलोकत पिय के नयन बने यों ।
बहुत शरद शशि मांझ अर वर द्वे चकोर ज्यों ॥84॥

*sabake mukha avalokata piya ke nayana bane yõ,*
*bahuta śarada śaśi mãjha ara vara dve cakora jyõ* (84)

As he gazes at them all,
admiring their lovely visage,
his eyes appear to be such.
That amidst many autumn moons,
sits a pair of partridge cakora,
which stares at the moon fondly,
always wanting for more.

अति आदर कर लई भर ठाडी चहुं दिश अनु ।
छबीली छिन मिले घेर मंजुल घन मूरत जनु ॥85॥

*ati ādara kara laī bhayī ṭhāḍi cahũ diśa anu,*
*chabīlī chaṭana mile ghera mañjula ghana mūrata janu* (85)

He meets and greets with great respect,
and they accept his extended hand.
Posing around him with style,
they swarm him as they stand.
Just like the bewitchingly beautiful thunderbolts,
cluster around a charming cloud.

नागर नगधर नंदचंद हसे मंदमंद तब ।
बोले बांके बेन प्रेम के परम एन सब ॥86॥

*nāgara naga-dhara nanda-canda hãnse manda-manda taba,*
*bole bãke bena prema ke parama ena saba* (86)

The suave Lord, the bearer of the Govaradhana mount,
and the moon of Nanda's house, then smiles slowly
on their account.
The words that he speaks are tricky or so,
but are the epitome of his supreme love though.

उज्ज्वल रस को यह स्वभाव बांकी छबि पावे ।
बंक कहन अरु चहन बंक अति रसहि बढावे ॥87॥

*ujjvala rasa ko yaha svabhāva bā̃ki chabi pāve,*
*baṅka kahana aru cahana baṅka ati rasahi baḍhāve* (87)

By its very nature, the radiating divine ecstasy
shines with the touch of trickery.
Tricky talk and artful amor,
wily words in perfect place,
as it all comes together,
their ecstasy is heightended for the better.

ये सब नवल किशोरी गोरी भरि प्रेम रस ।
ताते समुझ न परी करी पिय प्रेम विवश अस॥88॥

*ye saba navala kiśorī gorī bharī prema rasa,*
*tāte samujha na parī karī piya prema vivaśa asa* (88)

Filled with the ecstasy of love,
are these ever-young maidens fair,
with newly blooming youth,
they yet naïve and unaware.
And so, they fail to see,
blinded by their nescient despair,
that only out of pure love
he displayed his artful flair.

जैसे सुंदर नायक रूप गुण रसिक महा हे ।
सब गुण मिथ्या होय नेक जो वंक न चाहे ॥89॥

*jaise sundara nāyaka rūpa guṇa rasika mahā he,*
*saba guṇa mithyā hoya neka jo baṅka na cāhe* (89)

A handsome hero full of beauty and virtue,
and a savant of all ecstasy,
an aesthete of great value.
And yet, all his merits indeed go in vain,
if he views playful wiles with disdain.

कोउक वचन कहत नरम के उर संभार कर ।
कोउ कहे त्रिय धर्म भरम भेदक सुंदर वर ॥90॥

*koūka vacana kahata narama ke ura saṁbhāra kara,*
*koū kahe triya dharma bharama bhedaka sundara vara* (90)

Heedful not to hurt their heart,
and thus prudent and wary,
he talks with his tone soft,
watchfully wording his worry.
Rightful conduct fit for women,
he vouches like a wordsmith.
Prompting them of impropriety,
he pierces their myth.

लाल रसाल के बंक वचन सुन चकित भइ यों ।
बाल मृगीन की माल सघन वन भूल परी ज्यों ॥91॥

*lāla rasāla ke baṅka vacana suna cakita bhayī yõ,*
*bāla mṛgīna kī māla saghana bana bhūla parī jyõ* (91)

The lovely Lord whom they adore,
always sweet and pleasant,
hearing hurtful words from him
shocks them in that instant.
Like a flock of fawns
lost in a forest deep, afraid and meek,
so they stand there,
unable to speak.

मंद परस्पर हँसी लसी तिरछी अखियां अस ।
रूप उदधि इतराय रंगीली मीन पांत जस ॥92॥

*manda paraspara hãsī lasī tirachī akhiyā̃ asa,*
*rūpa udadhi itarāya raṅgīlī mīna-pā̃ta jasa* (92)

They arrive and softly smile,
simpering at one other,
and with arched angled eyes,
they peek all over.
They look like a shoal of flamboyant fish,
swimming in an ocean full of beauty.

Flaunting themselves with grace,
and a vague hint of vanity.

जब पिय कह्यो घर जाउ अधिक चित चिंता बाढी ।
पुतरिन की सी पांति रह गई इक टक ठाढी ॥93॥

*jaba piya kahyo ghara jāu adhika cita cintā bāḍhī,*
*putarina kī sī pā̃ti raha gayī ika ṭaka ṭhāḍhī* (93)

When their beloved asks them
to retreat to their home,
worries worsen in their minds,
as they lose all hope!
And so, they stand there stupefied,
staring like a statue,
stunned at his solemn stance,
and unable to argue.

दु:ख के बोझ छबि सीम ग्रीव नय चली नाल सी ।
अलक अलिन के भार नमित जानो कमल माल सी ॥94॥

*duḥkha ke bojha chabi sīma grīva naya calī nāla sī,*
*alaka alina ke bhāra namita jāno kamala māla sī* (94)

Weighed down with deep despair,
and head hung in sorrow,
flex of the neck is bent low,
like a stalk of lotus lined in tow.
Their lovely locks come dangling down,
like a line of black bees,
while their faces although in gloom,
look like lotus blooms.
And they pose together in a line,
like a garland of lotus skilfully aligned.

हिय भर विरह हुताश उसास निसंक आवत भर ।
चलहे कछुक मुरझाय मधु भरे अधर बिंब वर ।।95॥

*hiya bhara viraha hutāśa usāsa nisaṅka āvata bhara,*
*calahe kachuka murajhāye madhu bhare adhara biṁba vara* (95)

Hearts filled with the fire of separation,
they heave out a fearless sigh of chagrin.
Their nectar-filled sweet lips,
that look like a biṁba fruit,
seem to have somewhat withered away,
with the heat of their breath.

जब बोली ब्रजबाल लाल मोहन अनुरागी ।
सुंदर गद गद गिरा गिरिधरे मधुरी लागी ॥96॥

*jaba bolī brajabāla lāla mohana anurāgī,*
*sundara gada gada girā giridhare madhurī lāgī* (96)

When Braja women thus spoke,
filled with affection for dear Mohana
the Bearer of the Mount[20] was then touched
by their sweet voice, choked with emotion.

अहो मोहन अहो प्राणनाथ सुंदर सुखदायक ।
क्रूर वचन जिनि कहो नाहिं यह तुमरे लायक ॥97॥

*aho mohana aho prāṇanātha sundara sukha-dāyaka,*
*krūra vacana jina kaho nāhĩ yaha tumare lāyaka* (97)

O Mohana! O Lord of my life!
The beautiful one, the giver of all joys!
Do not speak words so cruel,
for it does not befit you.

जब कोउ पूछे धर्म ताहीसों कहिये पिय ।
विनहि पूछे धर्म कित कहिये दहिये हिय ॥98॥

20 The "Bearer of the Mount" is a literal translation of Giridhara, a name given to Kṛṣṇa in reference of the episode in which he lifted the mount Govaradhana to save the people of Braja from torrential rain.

*jaba koū pūche dharma tāhīsõ kahiye piya,*
*vinahi pūche dharma kita kahiye dahiye hiya* (98)

O Beloved! The righteous conduct
should never be breached.
However, only if one asks for it
should it be preached.
Why do tell us that which we do not seek?
Oh, it singes our hearts as you speak!

धर्म नेम जप तप व्रत सबको फलहि बतावे ।
यह कहूं नाहिन सुनी फलहि फिर धर्म सिखावे ॥99॥

*dharma nema japa tapa vrata sabako phala hi batāve,*
*yaha kahũ nāhina sunī phala hi phira dharma sikhāve* (99)

You are the fruit of righteous conduct and devout resolves,
of devotional repetitions, arduous practices, and pious vows.
But, never have we ever heard
that the fruit of all righteous paths
leads one back to the path again.

और तुम्हारो यह रूप धर्म के धर्म हि मोहे ।
धरमन के तुम धर्म भरम यह आगें कोहे ॥100॥

*aur tumhāro yaha rūpa dharma ke dharma hi mohe,*
*dharamana ke tuma dharma bharama yaha āgẽ kohe* (100)

And this form of yours
can enchant the right out of the righteousness.[21]
As you alone are the right amongst all the righteous deeds,
and the rest is just untruths that mislead.

तेसिय पिय की मुरली जिरली अधरसुधा रस।
सुन निज धर्म न तजे तरुणी त्रिभुवन में को अस ॥101॥

21 I have used the word "righteousness" for *dharma* here because although playfully, Kṛṣṇa righteously preaches to the *gopikās* about the moral code of conduct and this verse is the *gopikās*' response to it.

*tesiya piya ki muralī juralī adhara-sudha rasa,*
*suna nija dharma na taje taruṇī tribhuvana me ko asa* (101)

And so is the flute of the beloved,
as it meets his lips full of ecstatic nectar.
Will you ever find a young lady in the three worlds
unwilling to give up her virtue on hearing its word?

नगन खगन को मृगन को केसो धर्म रह्यो हे ।
छाने व्हे रहो पियन अब कछू जात क्यो है ॥102॥

*nagana khagana ko mṛgana ko keso dharma rahyo he,*
*chane vhe raho piyana aba kachu jata kahyo he* (102)

The stones, birds, and animals of the wild,[22]
have all lost their way of life.[23]
Hush now, O beloved,
for there is nothing more that we can say.

यह तुझारे करकमल महा दूती जो मुरली।।
राखे किनके धर्म अवर अधरनसूं जुरली।।१०३।।

*yaha tujhāre kara-kamala mahā dūtī jo muralī,*
*rākhe kinake dharma avara adharan sū̃ juralī* (103)

This flute you hold
in your lotuslike hands
is a great messenger!
Once it meets your divine lips,
whose virtue does it really keep?

नगन के धर्म न रहे पुलक तन चले ठोरतें ।
खग मृग गौ वच्छ मच्छ कच्छ ते रहे कोरतें ॥104॥

22 Mṛgana is a plural of Mṛga, which literally means a deer but is often used to denote animals of the wild in general.

23 In this verse, I have taken the word dharma to mean "way of life," as it is one of the many meanings associated with the word. Contextually, way of life for the wild, i.e. the law of the jungle, suits the verse better than other translations like "virtue" or "code of conduct" that are apt to denote societal constraints on the women in the previous verses.

*nagana ke dharma na rahe pulaka tana cale ṭhora te,*
*khaga mṛga gou baccha maccha kaccha te rahe kora te* (104)

The stones begin to flow from their resting place,
losing their natural way,
thrilled at the sound, and melting with joy,
slowly they move away!
The animals and the birds,
the cows and their calves,
fishes, tortoises, and the rest,
come around to gather, unafraid together,
at riverbank and the edge of the forest.

सुंदर पिय को बदन निरखके को नहिं भूले ।
रूप सरोवर मांझ अंबुज जनु फूले ॥105॥

*sundara piya ko badana nirakhake ko nahĩ bhūle,*
*rūpa sarovara mā̃jha śarada aṁbuja janu phūle* (105)

Who would not forget themselves
once they see our beautiful beloved!
Like a lotus blooming in autumn,
amidst a pond of beauty and blossom.

कुटिल अलक मुख कमल मानो मधुकर मतवारे ।
तिनमें मिल गये चपल नयन मन मधुप हमारे ॥106॥

*kuṭila alaka mukha kamala māno madhukara matavāre,*
*tinamẽ mila gaye capala nayana mana madhupa hamāre* (106)

Curly hair, falling to your lotuslike face,
looks like befuddled black bees.
With them join our fickle eyes and thirsty mind,
turning into honeybees.

चितवन मोहन मंत्र भ्रोंह जानो मन्मथ फांसी ।
निपट ठगोरी अहि मंद मृदु मादिक हांसी ॥107॥

*citavana mohana mantra bhrõha jāno manmatha phā̃sī,*
*nipaṭa ṭhagorī ahi manda mṛdu mādika hā̃si* (107)

Your glance casts a bewitching spell,
and your brows can trap the god of love.
But your intoxicating subtle, sweet smile
is the trickiest of all tricksters above!

अधर सुधा के लोभ भई हम दासी तिहारी ।
ज्यों लब्धी पद कमला नवला चंचल नारी ॥108॥

*adhara-sudhā ke lobha bhayī hama dāsī tihārī,*
*jyõ labdhī pada kamalā navalā cañcala nārī* (108)

Craving for the nectar of your lips, O lord,
we turned ourselves in your thrall.
Just as Lakṣmī, the wondrous beauty,
the capricious lady who craves your feet,
stays steadfast forever at your feet.

जो न देहो अधरामृत तो सुनहो सुंदर हरि ।
करहों यह तन भस्म विरह पावक में कूद परि ॥109॥

*jo na deho adharāmṛta to sunaho sundara hari,*
*karahõ yaha tana bhasma viraha pāvaka mẽ kūda pari* (109)

If you deprive us, O beautiful Hari,
of the nectar of your lips.
Diving into the fire of separation,
we will burn our bodies to ashes!

पुन पिय पदवी पाय बहुर धर हें सुंदर अंग ।
निधरक व्हे यह अधरामृत पीवत फिरहें संग ॥110॥

*puna piya padavī pāya bahura dhara hẽ sundara aṅga,*
*nidharaka vhe yaha adharāmṛta pīvata phirahẽ saṅga* (110)

Meditating on your beautiful form,
if we give our lives away,
we will attain, for sure,

your divine abode pure.
Unabashed then, we will wander with you,
and sip the nectar of your lips.

सुन गोपिन के प्रेम वचन आचसी लागी जिय ।
पिघल चल्यो नवनीत मीत नवनीत सदृश हिय ॥111॥

*suna gopina ke prema vacana ā̃casī lāgī jiya,*
*pighala calyo navanīta mīta navanīta sadṛśa hiya* (111)

Hearing the words full of love said by the herd-girls,
his heart seemed on fire.
And butter-like soft heart then melted like butter
with the heat of their arduous desire!

विहस मिले नंदलाल निरख ब्रजबाल विरह दु:ख ।
यद्यपि आत्माराम रमत भये जान अधिक सुख ॥112॥

*vihasa mile nandalāla nirakha brajabāla viraha duḥkha,*
*yadyapi ātmārāma ramata bhaye jāna adhika sukha* (112)

Seeing their sorrow of separation,
the son of Nanda embraced them with a smile.
One who plays with his own self alone
thus began his play with others,
for it's more joyful he learnt
than playing without the other!

विहरत विपिन विहार उदार रसिक नंदनंदन ।
नव कुंकुम घनसार चारु चरचत तन चंदन ॥113॥

*viharata vipina vihāra udāra rasika nandanandana,*
*nava kuṅkuma ghanasāra cāru caracata tana candana* (113)

They wander in the grove together,
with generous, ecstatic Son of Nanda.
They then anoint one another
with fresh musk, sandalwood, and camphor.

अद्‌त स्यामल रूप अंग बन्यो पीतवसन तनु ।
मूरत धरे श्रंगार प्रेम अंबर ओढे जनु ॥114॥

*adbhuta syāmala rūpa aṅga banyo pītavasana tanu,*
*mūrata dhare śṛṅgāra prema aṁbara oḍhe janu* (114)

His beautiful black body
is adorned with a yellow robe
as if passion personified and arose,
wearing a garment of love!

बिलुलित उर बनमाल लाल जब चलत चाल वर ।
कोटि मदन की भीर उठत छबि लुठत चरण तर ॥115॥

*bilulita ura banamāla lāla jaba calata cāla vara,*
*koṭi madana kī bhīra uṭhata chabi luṭhata caraṇa tara* (115)

The garland of wildflowers sways on his chest,
as the Lord walks with a charming gait.
Millions of gods of love rise and surge,
and forage at his feet,
to attain the splendour that lies underneath!

ब्रजयुवती कर मंडल मोहनलाल फिरत वन ।
अपनी द्‌ति के उजरे उडुपति जानो खेलत घन ॥116॥

*braja yuvatī kara maṇḍala mohanalāla phirata vana,*
*apanī dyuti ke ujare uḍupati jāno khelata ghana* (116)

The Braja women join their hands,
forming a divine circle on the land.
In the middle stands their dear Mohana;
this way they wander the woods together!
As if the moon plays amidst the clouds,
lit by his own light, shining abound!

कुंजन कुंजन डोलत जानो घन ते घन आवत ।
लोचन तृषित चकोरन के चित चोंप बढावत ॥117॥

*kuñjana kuñjana ḍolata jāno ghana te ghana āvata,*
*locana tṛṣita cakorana ke cita coṁpa baḍhāvata* (117)

From grove to grove they go,
like the moon goes from cloud to cloud.
Just as the partridges gaze at the moon
with their thirsting eyes,
so do the Braja women gaze at him,
as the love in their hearts intensifies!

सुभग सरिता के तीर धीर बलवीर गये तहां ।
कोमल मलय समीर छबि की महाभीर जहां ॥118॥

*subhaga saritā ke tīra dhīra balavīra gaye tahā̃,*
*komala malaya samīra chabina kī mahā-bhīra jahā̃* (118)

The gallant noble Hero then arrives
at the shore of the auspicious river![24]
Where the soft breeze blows,
fragrant with sandal,
and the beauties of all kinds
appear there personified!

कुसुम धूर धूंधर कुंज छबि पुंजन छाई ।
गुंजत मंजु अलिगण वेणु जनु बजत सुहाई ॥119॥

*kusuma dhūra dhū̃dhara kuñja chabi puñjana chāī,*
*guñjata mañju aligaṇa veṇu janu bajata suhāī* (119)

As the pollen from the flowers showers all around,
the misty grove radiates with beauty abound!
In it the bees buzz away in harmony,
as a flute is played with pleasing sound!

इत मकलत मालती चारू चपंक चित चोरत ।
उत घनसार तुसार मिलि मंदार झकोरत ॥120॥

*ita makalata mālatī cāru caṁpaka cita corata,*
*uta ghanasāra tusāra mili mandāra jhakorata* (120)

24 "Auspicious river" is a reference to river Yamunā, who is considered as the fourth consort of Kṛṣṇa and epitome of pure, unadulterated love (*nirguṇa-bhakti*) in the Vallabha tradition.

As fragrant Mālatī sways with joy,
Campā steals the hearts here!
And the cool aroma of the camphor
shakes the mighty mount Mandāra there![25]

इत लवंग नवरंग एलची झेलरही रस।।
उत कुरबक केवरो केतकी गंध बंध वस।।१२१।।

*ita lavaṅga navaraṅga elacī jhela rahī rasa,*
*uta kurabaka kevaro ketakī gandha bandha vasa* (121)

Luscious cardamoms are filled with sap,
and cloves adopt a new colour.
The fragrant flowers of Kurabaka, Kevarā, and Ketakī[26]
then enthrall with their alluring odour!

इत तुलसी छबि हुलसी छांडत परमल लपटे ।
उत कमोद आमोद मोद भरभर सुख दपटे ॥122॥

*ita tulasī chabi hulasī chā̃ḍata paramala lapaṭe,*
*uta kamoda āmoda moda bhara-bhara sukha dapaṭe* (122)

Wafts of their aroma flow all over,
as ravishing Tulasīs radiate and rejoice.[27]
And lovely lilies full of love,
are then filled with joy!

विलसत विविध विलास हास कर सूं कुच परसत ।
तरसत प्रेम अनंग रंग नवघन ज्यों बरसत ॥123॥

*vilasata vividha vilāsa hāsa kara sū̃ kuca parasata,*
*tarasata prema anaṅga raṅga navaghana jyõ barasata* (123)

25 Mālatī is a kind of jasmine with white flowers which bloom in the evening and Campā is a fragrant yellow blossom.

26 Kurabaka is a name for crimson amaranths, while Kevarā and Ketakī are fragrant flowers of a kind of screwpine trees.

27 Tulasī, often deified as a goddess who according to the Purāṇas married Lord Viṣṇu, is a kind of Indian basil significantly used in Vaiṣṇava liturgical traditions.

They stroll in varying groves and woods,
gardens and bays full of blossoms,
laughing with joy as he touches
their beautiful bosoms.
The god of love yearns for love,
as the colourful rain showers
from the new cloud above![28]

फूलन माल बनाय लाल पहरत पहरावत ।
सुमन सरोज सुधारत ओज मनोज बढावत ॥124॥

*phūlana māla banāya lāla paharata paharāvata,*
*sumana saroja sudhārata oja manoja baḍhāvata* (124)

Making garlands out of flowers,
they adorn each other!
And the god of love is filled with love
when the Lord aligns the flowers in order!

उज्वल मृदुल बालुका कोमल सुभग सुहाई ।
श्रीयमुनाजू निज तरंग करसों जु बनाई ॥125॥

*ujjvala mṛdula bālukā komala subhaga suhāī,*
*śrī-yamunājū nija taraṅga karasõ ju banāī* (125)

Bright, supple, and pleasing
are the soft grains of sand.
As the auspicious Yamunā made them
with her wavy watery hands!

तब आयो यह काम पंचशर कर हें जाके ।
ब्रह्मादिक कों जीत बढ रह्यो अति मद ताके ॥126॥

*taba āyo yaha kāma pañca-śara kara hẽ jāke,*
*brahmādika kõ jīta baḍha rahyo ati mada tāke* (126)

28 The "new cloud" is a metaphor for Kṛṣṇa as he is frequently associated with the colour of a raincloud owing to his dark complexion.

Then arrives the lord of love;
desire itself in person
brought along his five arrows,
that herald utter destruction![29]
Winning over Brahmā[30] and other gods alike,
filled up with great pride, he came over to strike!

निरख ब्रजबधू संग रंग भीने किशोर तन ।
आयो हरि मन्मथन उलट मथ्यो मनमथ को मन ॥127॥

*nirakha braja-badhū saṅga raṅga bhīne kiśora tana,*
*āyo hari manmatha ulaṭa mathyo manmatha ko mana* (127)

And then he saw the Braja women with the Lord,
immersed in the colours of his youthful body.
And so, Manmatha, the stirrer of hearts,
approached Hari to stir his heart.
But his game was turned over its head
when the stirrer of hearts
got his heart stirred instead!

मुरझ पर्यो तहां मैन कहूं धनुष कहूं विशिख वर ।
रति देखत पति दशा भीत भई मारत उर कर ॥128॥

*murajha paryo tahā̃ maina kahū̃ dhanuṣa kahū̃ viśikha vara,*
*rati dekhata pati daśā bhīta bhayī mārata ura kara* (128)

29 Traditionally it is believed that Kāmadeva, the god of love and desire, carries five arrows, namely, Unmada (enamourment), Sammohana (entrancement), Tapana (fiery feeling), Staṁbhana (paralysing), and Śoṣana (desiccation). As one is hit by each arrow, one is completely overcome by sensual desires leading to destruction. The reference to Kāma is crucial here, as Kāma believes this to be a worldly expression of love and hence, he arrives with his weapon of destruction. However, the humiliation of Kāma that will be described in the next few verses reiterates the emphasis laid on the fact that this is a divine union of individual selves with the Supreme Self. Thus, Kāma is vanquished here.

30 Brahmā is the god of creation, included in the Hindu trinity, which includes Viṣṇu (God of preservation) and Śiva (god of destruction). The Purāṇas state that Brahmā succumbed to his desires and Śiva destroyed them, after which, an ashamed Brahmā meditated for thousands of years to overcome his desires. This reference outlines the fact that even gods are not untouched by the power of Kāma, and yet, he fails to trap the women of Braja who are devoted to Kṛṣṇa.

And so, withered away he lay there,
with his bow and arrows scattered everywhere.
When Rati[31] saw her lord's plight,
she beat her breasts, scared by the sight!

पुन पुन पिय आलिंगत रोवत अति अनुरागी ।
मदन को वदन चुवाय अमृत भुज भर ले भागी ॥129॥

*puna-puna piya āliṅgata rovata ati anurāgī,*
*madana ko vadana cuvaya amṛta bhuja bhara le bhāgī* (129)

Filled with love for the lord of love,
with teary eyes, she embraced him,
again, and yet again.
Clasping him close to her body,
she fled from there,
carrying him in her ambrosian arms!

अस अद्‌त मोहनपिय सों मिली गोप दुलारी ।
अचरज नाहिन गर्व होय गिरधरजू की प्यारी ॥130॥

*asa adbhuta mohana-piya sõ milī gopa dulārī,*
*acaraja nāhina garva hoya giridharajū ki pyārī* (130)

And this is how the girls,
the endearing cowherds,
met dear Mohana,
their wonderful beloved!
Not surprising is their pride,
for they are truly adored
by the Bearer of the Mount,
the divine Lord!

रूप भरी गुण भरी भरी पुन परम प्रेम रस ।
क्यों न करे अभिमान कान्ह मोहन जिनके वस ॥131॥

*rūpa bharī guṇa bharī bharī puna parama prema rasa,*
*kyõ na kare abhimāna kānha mohana jinake vasa* (131)

31 Rati, which literally means love, is the wife of the lord of love, Kāmadeva.

Full of beauty and full of attributes,
and then they are filled
with the ecstasy of highest love!
So, why will they not be proud of their art?
Having charmed the charming Kānhā,
who is the charmer of all hearts!

जहां नदी नीर गंभीर तहां भले भंवरा परहीं ।
जलछल सलिलन परे परे तो छबि नहीं करहीं ॥132॥

*jahā̃ nadī nīra gaṁbhīra tahā̃ bhale bhãvarā parahī̃,*
*jala chala salilana pare pare to chabi nahī̃ karahī̃* (132)

Whirling pools befit the streams
only if the water runs deep.
In shallow waters they are not found,
and if they appear,
they seem unsuited and unsound![32]

प्रेमपुंज वरधन के काज ब्रजराज कुंवर पिय ।
मंजु कुंज में तनक दुरे अति प्रेम भरे हिय ॥133॥

*prema-puñja varadhana ke kāja braja-rāja kũvara piya,*
*mañju kuñja mẽ tanaka dure ati prema bhare hiya* (133)

To enhance the lustre of love,
the king of Braja, the dear Lord,
hides away in the alluring grove,
with his heart full of intense love![33]

32 This metaphor is used to outline the idea that only if one has devotion of the highest order for the supreme Lord, like the *gopikās*, does one's pride seem appropriate. Otherwise, it is ill-suited. Instrestingly, the pride of the *gopikās* is often defined as an inappropriate act, a lesson in what not to do in an ideal act of devotion, by both the *Bhāgavata* and Vallabha's commentary. However, Viṭṭhalanātha strongly defends the *gopikās* here by asserting that it is not pride, but an expression of the highest order of love and should not be emulated by ordinary devotees. As Nandadāsa is a disciple of Viṭṭhalanātha, it can be said that he is following his guru's commentary by similarly defending the *gopikās* here instead of condemning their pride as the *Bhāgavata* does.

33 In sync with the previous verse, Nandadāsa presents the disappearance of Kṛṣṇa in a positive light. While it is often seen as a consequence of inappropriate pride of the *gopikās*, here, it is explained as a tool used by Kṛṣṇa to enhance their love, as love is intensified in absence.

इति रासक्रीडा वर्णने प्रथमोऽध्यायः ॥1॥

|| *iti rāsakrīḍā varṇane prathamo'dhyāyaḥ* ||

So ends, the first chapter describing the play of *rāsa*.

Similar ideas are expressed in the succeeding verses, which convey through different metaphors that separation is just another and arguably more intense flavour of love.

FOUR

# Chapter II: Pangs of Separation

## Verses 134–180

मधुर वस्तु जो खाय निरंतर सुख तो भारी ।
विच विच अमल कटु तिक्त जो अति रुचिकारी ॥134॥

*madhura vastu jo khāya nirantara sukha to bhārī,*
*vica vica amala kaṭu tikta jo ati rucikārī* (134)

Every day one who eats
a fare full of sweets
attains great pleasure indeed.
Yet, every now and then,
a dash of bitter, spicy, and sour
enhances the taste of sweetness!

ज्यों पट पुट के दिये निपट अति रस ही बढे रंग ।
तेसें रंचक विरह प्रेम के पुंज बढे अंग ॥135॥

*jyõ paṭa puṭa ke diye nipaṭa ati rasa hi baḍhe raṅga,*
*tesẽ rañcaka viraha prema ke puñja baḍhe aṅga* (135)

Just as a garment, coloured nice,
glistens even more when dyed twice!
So does love shine brighter,
when hued with a little separation.

जिनके नयन निमेष ओट कोटिक युग जाही ।
तिनकूं गहवर कुंज ओट दु:ख गनना नाही ॥136॥

*jinake nayana nimeṣa oṭa koṭika yuga jāhī,*
*tinakū̃ gahavara kuñja oṭa duḥka gananā nāhī̃* (136)

A blink of an eye that shields him away
seems like aeons and aeons have gone by.
When the deep woods veil him for good,
what must they feel and where must they go?
Oh! who can account for their sorrow?

ठगी सी रही ब्रजबाल लाल गिरधर पिय बिन यों ।
निधन महा धन पाय बहुर फिर जाय भई त्यों ॥137॥

*ṭhagī sī rahī braja-bāla lāla-giridhara piya bina yõ,*
*nidhana mahā dhana pāya bahura phira jāya bhayī tyõ* (137)

The women of Braja, without Lord Giridhara,
stand and stare, stunned as he disappeared!
Just like a pauper who finds
great wealth without measure,
then it is snatched away,
and he loses all his treasure.

व्हे गई विरह विकल बूझत द्रुम वेली वन ।
को जड को चैतन्य कछु न जानत विरही जन ॥138॥

*vhe gayī viraha vikala būjhata druma velī vana,*
*ko jaḍa ko caitanya kachu na jānata virahī jana* (138)

Forlorn with grief they ask,
shrubs, creepers, and vines of the forest.
The forsaken women grieve in despair,
and soon become unaware
of what is sentient and what is not!

हे मालती हे जातियूथ के सुन दे हित चित ।
मान हरन मन हरन लाल गिरिधरन लहे इत ॥139॥

*he mālati he jāti-yūtha ke suna de hita cita,*
*māna harana mana harana lāla-giridharana lahe ita* (139)

O Mālati, and all in your troop,
tell us something that soothes our hearts too!
Have you seen our dear Giridhara,
he who snatched our pride and snatched our hearts?

हे केतकी इततें चितये कितहू पिय रूसे ।
किधों नंदनंदन मंद मुसक तिहारे मन मूंसे ॥140॥

*he ketakī ita te citaye kitahū piya rūse,*
*kidhõ nandanandana manda musaka tihāre mana mūse* (140)

Tell us, O Ketakī! have you seen him come this way,
our displeased beloved who went away?
Or did the lovely Son of Nanda,
with his soft smile anew,
snare your hearts too?

हे मुक्ताफल वेली धरें मुक्ताफल माला ।
कहूं देखे नयन विशाल मोहन नंद के लाला ॥141॥

*he muktāphala velī dharẽ muktāphala mālā,*
*kahū̃ dekhe nayana viśāla mohana nanda ke lālā* (141)

O you vines! With pearly white flowers,
he wears a garland made of your flowers.
The one with big, lovely eyes,
our dear Mohana!
Did you see him?
The charming Son of Nanda!

हे मंदार उदार बीर करबीर महामति ।
देखे कहूं बलबीर धीर मन हरन धीर गति ॥142॥

*he mandāra udāra bīra karabīra mahāmati,*
*dekhe kahū̃ balabīra dhīra mana harana dhīra gati* (142)

O mighty Mandāra! The generous one!
O Oleander![34] The wise one!
Did you see our valorous Balabīra,
that skilful snatcher of hearts!

हे चंदन दुःखकंदन सबकी जरन सिरावहू ।
नंदनंदन जगवंदन चंदन हमहि बतावहू ॥143॥

*he candana duḥkha-kandana sabakī jarana sirāvahū,*
*nandanandana jagavandana candana hamahi batāvahū* (143)

O Sandal, the one who soothes all sorrows,
the one who calms the burns of all.
Where is the son of Nanda, who is revered by all kinds?
Tell us and calm our minds!

बूझोरी इन लतन फूल रही फूलन जोइ ।
सुंदर पिय के परस बिना यह फूल न होइ ॥144॥

*būjhorī ina latana phūla rahī phūlana joī,*
*sundara piya ke parasa binā yaha phūla na hoī* (144)

Ask these blossoming vines,
blooming full of flowers.
Without our beautiful beloved touching you,
these flowers would not have bloomed!

हे सखी यह मृगवधू इनको पूछे अनुसरि ।
डहडहें इनके नयन अबहि कहूं देखे हे हरि ॥145॥

*he sakhī yaha mṛga-vadhū ina ko pūche anusari,*
*Ḍahaḍahẽ inake nayana aba hi kahū̃ dekhe haĩ hari* (145)

O friend, look at the deer-wives,
question these pretty hinds!
Their eyes are lit with love,
blissful all along,

34 The word *karavīra* that appears in the main verse is a name for yellow oleander. It is commonly known as *kaner* in Hindi.

for they have seen our Hari,
not before long!

अहो सुभग वन सुगंध पवन नेसिक थिर रहि चलि ।
सुख के भवन दु:ख दवन रवन कहूं इत चितये बलि ॥146॥

*aho subhaga vana sugandha pavana nesika thira rahi cali,*
*sukha ke bhavana duḥkha davana ravana kahū̃ ita citaye bali* (146)

O auspicious, fragrant breeze of the grove,
stay still for a moment!
O brave one! Have you seen him?
He who quells our woes and delights in us,
and he who is the palace of blissfulness!

अहो कदंब अहो अंब नीम क्यों रहे मोन गहि ।
अहो वट तुंग सुरंग भीर कहूं ते इत उत लहि ॥147॥

*aho kadaṁba aho aṁba nīma kyõ rahe mona gahi,*
*aho vaṭa tuṅga suraṅga bhīra kahū̃ tẽ ita uta lahi* (147)

O Kadaṁba tree! O Mango and Nīma!
what is this silence for?
O brave, beautiful, and big Banyan tree!
Have you seen him somewhere around here?

अहो असोक हर सोक लोकमनि पियहि बतावहु ।
अहो फनस शुभ सनस मरत त्रिय अमृत प्यावहु ॥148॥

*aho asoka hara soka lokamani piyahi batāvahu,*
*aho phanasa śubha sanasa marata triya amṛta pyāvahu* (148)

O Asoka, you who are devoid of woe,
take away our sorrow,
please tell us about our dear beloved,
who is the jewel of the world.
O Jackfruit, the auspicious fruit,
we are dying, do you not see?

By uniting us with our ambrosia,
cut our woes at the root!

यमुना निकट के विटप पूछ भई निपट उदासी ।
क्यों कहि हे सखी कठिन तीरथ के वासी ॥149॥

*yamunā nikaṭa ke viṭapa pūcha bhayī nipaṭa udāsī,*
*kyõ kahi he sakhī mahā kaṭhina tīratha ke vāsī* (149)

And so they rest, in great distress,
calling to the trees on the bank of Yamunā!
Why would they answer us, they say,
for cruel are they for sure
who reside at the holy shore!

अहो कमल शुभ करन वरन कहूं तें हरि निरखे ।
कमलमाल वनमाल कमलकर अति हि हरखे ॥150॥

*aho kamala śubha karana varana kahū̃ te hari nirakhe,*
*kamalamāla vanamāla kamalakara ati hi harakhe* (150)

O Lotus! the bestower of fortune,
he is just like you, did you see?
Our dearest Hari, where is he?
He is delightful just like you,
holding your flower in his hands,
wearing a garland made of you!

अहो अवनी नवनीत चोर चित चोर हमारे ।
राखे किते दुराय बताय देहु प्राण पियारे ॥151॥

*aho avanī navanīta cora cita cora hamāre,*
*rākhe kite durāya batāya dehu prāṇa piyāre* (151)

O Earth! you know our butter-thief,
the root of our grief,
for just like he stole the butter,
he stole our minds!
Yet, he is dearer than our lives.

Oh, is he with you?
Tell us where you hide him without ado!

हे तुलसी कल्याणी सदा गोविंद पद प्यारी ।
क्यों न कहो सखी नंद सुवन सों दशा हमारी ॥152॥

*he tulasī kalyāṇī sadā govinda pada pyārī,*
*kyõ na kaho sakhī nanda suvana sõ daśā hamārī* (152)

O Tulasī, the blessed one!
you are the one who Govinda adores,
and the one who adores the feet of our Lord!
O my friend, look at our sight,
why do you not tell that sweet son of Nanda,
about our pitiable plight?

जहां आवत तम पुंज कुंज गहबर तरु छाई ।
अपने मुख चांदने चलत सुंदरी तिहिं माई ॥153॥

*jahā̃ āvata tama puñja kuñja gahabara taru chāī,*
*apane mukha cāndane calata sundarī tihĩ māī* (153)

And so they go, in great sorrow,
from one deep dark grove to another,
filled with trees, dense and deep,
spread all over.
But what a beauty they all are,
with moonlike faces that shine like moons!
and following the light it casts,
they walk through the thick of the woody paths!

यह विध वन घन ढूंढ बूझ उनमत की नांई ।
करन लगी मन हरन लाल लीला मन भाई ॥154॥

*yaha vidha vana ghana dū̃ḍha būjha unmata kī nā̃ī,*
*karana lagī mana harana lāla līlā mana bhāī* (154)

In this way they wander
into the thick woods yonder,

in vain they try to ask and find,
but so they appear in the end
like the one who has lost their mind!
In frenzy they go, trying to echo
the divine plays of their dear Lord,
they choose to enact and put up an act
of the ones they adore to their heart's core!

मोहन लाल रसाल की लीला इनही सोहे ।
केवल तनमय भई कछु न जाने हम कोहे ॥155॥

*mohana lāla rasāla kī līlā inahī sohe,*
*kevala tanamaya bhayī kachū na jāne hama kohe* (155)

The plays of dear Mohana,
their ecstatic mate,
suit them well when they imitate.
And so they lose their selves
in his divine deeds;
Forgetting who they are,
they are immersed in him indeed!

हरि की सी चलन बिलोकन हरि की सी बोलन हेरनि ।
हरि की सी गायन घेरन टेरन चहूं पट फेरनि ॥156॥

*hari kī-sī calana bilokana hari kī-sī bolana herani,*
*hari kī-sī gāyana gherana ṭerana cahū̃ paṭa pherani* (156)

Like Hari they walk and like Hari they gaze,
beholding like him as they engage.
Like Hari they sing, calling for cows,
and like him they gather around;
with the stroke of their garment, they caress the cows.

हरि की सी बन तें आवन गावन अति रस रंगी ।
हरि की सी कौतुक रचन नचन नित ललित त्रिभंगी ॥157॥

*hari kī-sī bana te āvana gāvana ati rasa raṅgī,*
*hari kī-sī kautuka racana nacana nita lalita tribhaṅgī* (157)

The arrival of Hari from the forest,
they enact and imitate.
His colourful song ecstatic,
they sing to echo his trait.
To create his joyous sport,
like Hari they dance;
posing their body in a triple-bend,[35]
they attain his sublime stance!

कोउ गिरिवर अंबर को कर धर बोलत हें तब ।
निडर इनहिं तर रहो ग्वाल गोपी गायन सब ॥158॥

*koū girivara aṁbara ko kara dhara bolata hẽ taba,*
*niḍara inahī̃ tara raho gvāla gopī gāyana saba* (158)

Using her robe like the King of the Mountains,[36]
one of them proceeds to announce,
O men and women of the cowherd folk,
cows and animals alike, do not be afraid of the strike,
take shelter and do not doubt,
come under this mighty Govaradhana mount!

भ्रंगी भजे ते भ्रंग होय यह कीट महाजड ।
कृष्णप्रेम ते कृष्ण होय कछु नाहीं अचरज बड ॥159॥

*bhraṅgī bhaje te bhraṅga hoya yaha kīṭa mahajaḍa,*
*kṛṣṇa-prema tẽ kṛṣṇa hoya kachu nahī̃ acaraja baḍa* (159)

A bug, bewitched by a buzzing bee,
although insentient and dense,
is devoted nonetheless,

35 Triple-bend is my translation of the word "*tribhaṅgī,*" which is a standing pose found in many classical dances in India. As the name suggests, the shoulders and neck are bent in one direction, while the hips are bent in another direction and the knees are yet again bent in the direction of the neck. This pose is traditionally associated with gracefulness, beauty, and limberness and is often found in classical art and sculptures in India. One common name for Kṛṣṇa is *lalita-tribhaṅgi,* which means one who looks pleasing in the triple-bend position.

36 I am using "king of the mount" to translate "*girivara,*" which is a common name for Govaradhana mountain that Kṛṣṇa lifted on his little finger to save Braja from the wrath of Indra. The *gopikā* here is enacting this exact episode from the *Bhāgavata* to relive some unforgettable moments they shared with Kṛṣṇa.

and so it turns into a bee itself![37]
So, by their love for Kṛṣṇa,
if they turn into Kṛṣṇa themselves,
immersed in his state,
it is not a surprise great.

जो रज अज कमला शिव खोजत योजत जोगी हिय ।
सो रज वंदन करन लगी सिर धरन लगी त्रिय ॥160॥

*jo raja aja kamalā śiva khojata yojata jogī hiya,*
*so raja vandana karana lagī sira dharana lagī triya* (160)

A mere speck of the dust from Braja
is yearned for by Brahmā and Kamalā,[38]
sought after by Śiva,
and meditated upon by yogis[39]
To that very dust the women of Braja
revere and bow,
by setting it on their brows.

जहां निरखे ढिंग जगजगात प्यारी पिय के पग ।
चित परस्पर चकिय भई जुर चली तिहिं मग ॥161॥

*jahā̃ nirakhe ḍhiṅga jagamagāta pyārī piya ke paga,*
*cita parspara cakita bhayī jura calī tihī̃ maga* (161)

And that is when they see at hand,
shimmering in the sand,
the footprints of their beloved and his dear love.[40]

---

37 A common lore in Hindu devotional tradition is of a kind of insect that gets intently attracted to the buzzing of a bee and eventually turns into the bee itself. This metaphor is always used to indicate the power of one-pointedness in both yogic and *bhakti* cultures, which can transform the meditator into the object of meditation.

38 Kamalā (one who is born of a lotus) is another name for Goddess Lakṣmī.

39 The reverence for the dust of Braja is widely present within the Kṛṣṇa devotional traditions due to the belief that Kṛṣṇa walked on Braja and continues to walk there even today. This sacred dust is even used as *caraṇāmṛta* (nectar of his divine feet), which is consumed by the devotees to cleanse themselves internally before they begin their daily worship.

40 According to the *Bhāgavata*, the *gopikās* see two set of footprints, one of Kṛṣṇa and the other of a mysterious, unnamed woman. Although the text does not identify her, the folklores from Braja assert they were the trails of Kṛṣṇa's eternal love, Rādhā. Staying true to the parent text,

Astonished, they look at each other,
and from that place they proceed ahead together.

चकित भई सब कहे कोन यह बडभागिन अस ।
परमकांत एकांत पाय पीबत जु अधर रस ॥162॥

*cakita bhayī saba kahe kona yaha baḍa-bhāgina asa,*
*parama-kā̃nta ekā̃nta pāya pībata ju adhara rasa* (162)

Who is the greatly blessed lady?
they ask each other in dismay.
She is drinking the ambrosia of his lips,
finding our dearest love alone in this way!

पुन आगे चल अवलोकी नव पल्लव श्रेणी ।
जहां पिय कुसुम ले सुहस्त सों गूंथी बेणी ॥163॥

*puna āge cala avalokī nava pallava śreṇī,*
*jahā̃ piya kusuma le suhasta sõ gū̃thī beṇī* (163)

Led by the trail, they arrive at a scene
where they see a vine with new blossoms.
Here is where our dear love,
with his graceful divine hands,
braided flowers in her hair!

तहां पायो एक मंजु मुकुर मणि जटित बिलोलें ।
तिहिं बूझत ब्रजबाल विरह भर्यो सोउ न बोले ॥164॥

*tahā̃ pāyo eka mañju mukura maṇi-jaṭita bilolẽ,*
*tihī̃ būjhata braja-bāla viraha bharyo soū na bole* (164)

There they found, lying on the ground,
a magnificent mirror, with dangling jewels.
Then the women of Braja ask the mirror,
about their dear Lord.

---

Nandadāsa too has refrained from revealing her in this rendition, although he does refer to her as "*pyārī*." While *pyārī* has a range of meanings, such as adorable, dear, or love, it is also a popular word used for Rādhā in the *aṣṭa-chāpa* compositions. Yet, the context in which Nandadāsa is using it cannot be stated contextually.

But forlorn from separation and filled with despair,
he lay silent there.

तर्क करत आपस में अहो यह क्यों कर लीनो ।
तिनमें को तिन के हिय की जिन उत्तर दीनो ॥165॥

*tarka karata āpasa mẽ aho yaha kyõ kara līno,*
*tinamẽ ko tina ke hiya kī jina uttara dīno* (165)

They reason amongst themselves,
trying to find,
oh, why did he hold the mirror in his hands,
what was in his mind?
As they surmise, a lady wise
begins to answer,
for she excelled in the art
of knowing her beloved's heart!

बेनी गुहन समय छबीले बैठे पीछे जब ।
सुंदर वदन बिलोकत सुख को अंतर भयो तब ॥166॥

*benī guhana samaya chabīle baithe pīche jaba,*
*sundara vadana bilokata sukha ko antara bhayo tab* (166)

As our charming love braided her hair,
behind her back he sat.
His beautiful body that she gazed at
was then veiled from her.
Thus, she was left, bereft and deprived,
of the bliss that pleased her eye!

ताते मंजुल मुकुर सुकर ले बाल दिखायो ।
श्रीमुख को प्रतिबिंब सखी तब सन्मुख आयो ॥167॥

*tāte mañjula mukura sukara le bāla dikhāyo,*
*śrī-mukha ko pratibiṁba sakhī taba sanamukha āyo* (167)

With his noble hands, he then showed her
this beautiful, bejewelled mirror!

His splendorous face reflected in it, and,
once again, he was before his friend!

धन्य कहत भई ताहि नाहिं कछु मन में कोपी ।
निरमत्सर जे संत तिनकी चूडामणि गोपी ॥168॥

*dhanya kahata bhayī tāhi nāhī̃ kachu mana mẽ kopī,*
*niramatsara je santa tinakī cūḍāmaṇi gopī* (168)

Blessed, oh blessed is she, they say,
not a hint of anger in their words.
Devoid of envy or pique, as they speak,
and nobler than the saints,
these cowherd women are indeed
crest jewel of the saints.

इन नीके आराधे हरि ईश्वर वर जोई ।
ताते अधर सुधारस निडरक पीवत सोई ॥169॥

*ina nīke ārādhe hari īśvara vara joī,*
*tāte adhara sudhārasa niḍaraka pīvata soī* (169)

They say together in accord,
she worshipped our Hari, our Lord,
with exceptional devotion and more!
And so without fear, she sits near,
drinking the ecstatic nectar pure,
from his lovely lips for sure.[41]

सोऊ पुनि अभिमान भरी तब कहन लगी त्रिय ।
मोते चल्यो न जात जहां तुम चलन कहत पिय ॥170॥

*soū puni abhimāna bharī taba kahana lagī triya,*
*mote calyo na jāta jahā̃ tuma calana kahata piya* (170)

41 Verses 168 and 169 reiterate the distinctive theme of Vallabhite perspective on *rāsa-līla* by asserting that love of the *gopikās* was neither ordinary nor sensual despite the way it is worded. The evident lack of envy bespeaks of their piety, and so does the fact that they attribute their proximity with the Lord to ultimate and pure devotion.

Alas! the lady sublime, she too succumbed to pride,
and with great vanity, she then spoke her mind.
Oh, I simply cannot walk anymore,
wherever, my beloved, you want me to go!

पुनि आगे चल तनक दूर देखी सोई ठाढी ।
जासों सुंदर नंदसुवन पिय अति रति बाढी ॥171॥

*puni āge cala tanaka dūra dekhī soī ṭhāḍhī,*
*jāsõ sundara nandasuvana piya ati rati bāḍhī* (171)

Standing by the way,
that very lady they see,
as a little ahead they proceed.
The one with whom the noble son of Nanda
enjoyed great pleasure,
and his love grew beyond measure!

गोरे तन की जोत छूट छबि छाय रही धर ।
मानो ठाढी कनक बेलि कंचन अवनी पर ॥172॥

*gore tana kī jota chūṭa chabi chāya rahī dhara,*
*māno ṭhāḍhī kanaka beli kañcana avanī para* (172)

Her body fair, flickers like a fiery flame,
the light of which lights the earth aflame!
As if a golden creeper stands,
glimmering on the golden land!

ज्यों घन ते बिछुरी बिजुरी नौतन छबि काछें ।
किधों चंद सों रूस चंद्रिका रहि गई पाछें ॥173॥

*jyõ ghana te bichurī bijurī nautana chabi kāchẽ,*
*kidhõ canda sõ rūsa candrikā rahi gayī pāchẽ* (173)

Like a thunderbolt that
separates from a rain cloud,
acquiring a new form,
she shimmers on the ground!

Or maybe like the moonlight, shining bright,
left behind by the moon, and upset with her celestial love,
she comes down on earth to bloom.

नयनन तें जल धार हार धोवत धर धावत ।
भ्रमर उडाय न सकत वास वस मुख ढिंग आवत ॥174॥

*nayanana te jala dhāra hāra dhovata dhara dhāvata,*
*bhramara uḍāya na sakata vāsa vasa mukha ḍhiṅga āvata* (174)

Tears flowing from her eyes
fall down to the ground,
soaking her necklace on their way.
And so, her fragrance spreads afar.
A bumble bee comes buzzing about,
tranced by her sweet scent;
near her face he flies around.

क्वासि क्वासि पिय महाबाहु यों वदत अकेली ।
महा विरह की ध्वनि सुन रोवत खग मृग वेली ॥175॥

*kvāsi kvāsi*[42] *piya mahābāhu yõ vadata akelī,*
*mahā viraha kī dhvani suna rovata khaga mṛga velī* (175)

O my beloved, one with long arms!
Where are you, where are you?
she uttered, forlorn in the woods.
The birds, animals, and vines,
watch her as she pines;
hearing her cries deep,
they all begin to weep.

42 The phrase *kvāsi-kvāsi,* in the main verse is a direct quote from the *Bhāgavata* (10.30.39), in which the *gopikās* hear Kṛṣṇa echoing this phrase along with them. It literally means "where is he, where is he" and is often used by the *aṣṭa-chāpas* in their compositions to reiterate the idea that Kṛṣṇa never really left the *gopikās*. In fact, he helped them to find himself and this suggests that the disappearance of Kṛṣṇa is a part of divine play designed to intensify their devotional experience.

ता सुंदरी की दशा देख कछु कहत न आवे ।
विरह भरी पूतरी होय तो कछु छबि पावे ॥176॥

*tā sundarī kī daśā dekha kachu kahata na āve,*
*viraha bharī pūtarī hoya to kachu chabi pāve* (176)

Oh, the plight of that beauty
cannot be expressed in words.
If there ever were a beautiful figure
made of lovelorn longing,
only would it then compare,
to this beauty's woeful affairs.

धाय भुजन भर लई सबन ले ले उर लाई ।
मानो महानिधि खोय मध्य आधी निधि पाई ॥177॥

*dhāya bhujana bhara laī sabana le le ura lāī,*
*māno mahā-nidhi khoya madhya ādhī nidhi pāī* (177)

Extending their arms, they race to embrace her,
and hold her close to their hearts.
After losing a treasure trove,
as if they find, amidst the grove,
a part of their lost treasure,
like half of their great pleasure!

कोउ चुंबत मुख कमल कोऊ भ्रू भाल सुअलकें ।
जिनमें पिय संगम की मंजुल श्रमजल झलकें ॥178॥

*koū cuṁbata mukhakamala koū bhrūbhāla su alakẽ,*
*jinamẽ piya saṅgama kī mañjula śramajala jhalakẽ* (178)

Some kiss her lotus face, other kiss her forehead,
one that is adorned, with lovely black hair.
On her beautiful brows, droplets of sweat shimmer,
and bespeak her desire to unite with her lover.

पोछत अपने अंचल रुचिर दृगंचल तियके ।
पीक भरे सु कपोल लोल रदक्षत सु पियके ॥179॥

*pochata apane añcala rucira dṛgañcala tiyake,*
*pīka bhare su kapola lola radakṣata su piya ke* (179)

With the end of their robes, some wipe her tears,
that flow from her pretty eyes.
Others wipe her damp cheeks,
which bear the mark of their beloved's kiss.

तिहिं ले तहां ते अवर बहुर यमुना तट आई ।
जहां नंदनंदन जगवंदन पिय लाड लडाई ॥180॥

*tihĩ le tahā̃ te avara bahura yamunā taṭa āī,*
*jahā̃ nandanandana jagavandana piya lāḍa laḍāī* (180)

Then they bring her back,
right to the shore of Yamunā.
For that is where the Son of Nanda,
revered by the world indeed,
was cherished by her lovable deeds.

इति रासक्रीडा वर्णने द्वितीयोऽध्याय

|| *iti rāsakrīḍā varṇane dvitīyo'dhyāyaḥ* ||

So ends, the second chapter describing the play of *rāsa*.

FIVE

# Chapter III: The Song of the *Gopikās*

Verses 181–195

कहन लगी अहो कुंवर कान्ह ब्रज प्रकटे जबतें ।
अवधिभूत इंदिरा अलंकृत होय रही तबतें ।।181।।

*kahana lagī aho kũvara kānha braja prakaṭe jaba te,*
*avadhibhūta indirā alaṅkṛta hoya rahī taba te* (181)

O Lord, our dear Kānhā,
the moment in which you appeared in Braja,
the lengths of this land are embellished
by the presence of Indirā[43] ever since!

सबन सो सब सुख बरखत शशि ज्यों बढत दिहारी ।
तिनमें यह पुन गोपवधु पिय निपट तिहारी ॥182॥

*sabana so saba sukha barakhata śaśi jyõ baḍhata dihārī,*
*tinamẽ yaha puna gopa-vadhu piya nipaṭa tihārī* (182)

Joys of all kinds shower on all,
increasing every day,
just like the new moon waxes
from the first lunar phase.
We the cowherd brides,
are dearest to you of them all,
as we are the ones you greatly adore.

43 An epithet for Goddess Lakṣmī.

नयन मूंदवो महा शस्त्र ले हांसी फांसी ।
मारत हो कित सुरतनाथ बिनमोल की दासी ॥183॥

*nayana mūndavo mahā śastra hā̃nsi phā̃nsī,*
*mārata ho kita suratanātha bina mola kī dāsī* (183)

You trap us by your smile,
the greatest weapon known to slay,
and then you turn your eyes away.
O lord of loving sports,
why do you slay us at all?
Serving you without a price,
are we not in your thrall?

विषजल हू ते व्याल अनल तें दामिनी झरतें ।
क्यों राखी नहीं मरन दई नागर नग धरतें ॥।184॥

*viṣajala hū te vyāla anala tẽ dāminī jharatẽ,*
*kyõ rākhī nahī̃ marana daī nāgara naga dharate* (184)

From the poisonous water and the fervent flame,
from the great serpent and his beastly bane,
from the thunderbolts and the roaring rain.[44]
Why not let us die?
O my suave Lord, the Bearer of the Mount!
Why keep us safe on all accounts?

जब तुम यशुदासुवन भये पिय अति इतराने ।
विश्व कुसल के काज विधना विनती कर आने ॥185॥

44 These are the references to three occasions out of many on which Kṛṣṇa saved the people of Braja from various kinds of evils. "Poisonous water" and "great serpent" refer to the story of Kāliyā-Mardana, in which a serpent with over a hundred hoods came to live in the river Yamunā and its poison began to kill animals and people of Braja. Kṛṣṇa fights the serpent and dances on its hoods to crush its ego (*Bhāgavata* 10.16). "Fervent flame" indicates the time when Kṛṣṇa swallowed a fierce forest fire to save his cows and cowherd friends (*Bhāgavata* 10.19). Lastly, "roaring rain" refers to the time when Kṛṣṇa stopped the worship of Indra, who is the rain-god and also the king of the gods. Enraged, Indra tried to flood Braja with rain but Kṛṣṇa lifted the mount Govaradhana with his little finger and provided shelter to everyone for seven days until Indra realised his folly and surrendered (*Bhāgavata* 10.25).

*jaba tuma yaśodāsuvana bhaye piya ati itarāne,*
*viśva kusala ke kāja vidhanā vinatī kara āne* (185)

Ever since you took birth
as lovely Yaśodā's son,
O my beloved swain,
you have become so vain!
Remember you came here on Brahmā's request
to sustain the world with your divine quest!

अहो मित्र अहो प्राणनाथ यह अचरज भारी ।
अपने जन कों मार करो किनकी रखवारी ॥186॥

*aho mitra aho prāṇanātha yaha acaraja bhārī,*
*apane jana kõ māra karo kinakī rakhavārī* (186)

O friend, O the Lord of our lives!
This is truly a great surprise!
Who are you planning to shelter
after you slay your own people?

जब पशुचारन चलत चरण कोमल धरत वन में ।
शिलतृण कंटक अटकत कसकत मन में ॥187॥

*jaba paśucārana calata caraṇa komala dharata vana mẽ,*
*Śila-tṛṇa kanṭaka aṭakata kasakata hamāre mana mẽ* (187)

When you walk barefoot grazing the cows,
and your soft feet rest on the forest land,
rocks, thorns, and stones then hurt you,
but they pierce our hearts too!

प्रणत मनोरथ करण चरण सरसी रुह पिय को ।
कहा घट जैहे नाथ हरत दुःख हमरे जिय के ॥188॥

*praṇata manoratha karaṇa caraṇa sarasī ruha piya ke,*
*kahā ghaṭa jaihe nātha harata duḥkha hamare jiya ke* (188)

O beloved, your lotuslike feet
fulfil the desires of all their devotees.

My lord, if you choose
to take away our sorrows too,
what will you really lose?

कहां हमारी प्रीत कहां तुमारी निठुराई ।
मणि पखान सो खचे दैव सो कछु न बस्याई ॥189॥

*kahā̃ hamārī prīta kahā̃ tumharī niṭhurāī,*
*maṇi pakhāna so khace daiva so kachu na basyāī* (189)

Look at our loveliness,
and look at your harshness!
As jewels studded in stone together
are coerced by fate to be together,
and spend eternity with each other!

जब तुम कानन जात सहस्त्र युग सम बीतत छिन ।
दिन बीतत जिहीं भांत हमहि जाने पिय तुम बिन ॥190॥

*jaba tuma kānana jāta sahastra yuga sama bītata china,*
*dina bītata jihī̃ bhā̃ta hamahi jāne piya tuma bina* (190)

When you go to the forest leaving us behind,
each moment feels like ages have gone by.
The time we spend without you, O Beloved,
only we know how each of our days go.

जब कानन ते आवत सुंदर आनन देखे ।
तब यह बिधना क्रूर करी घर नयन निमेखे ॥191॥

*jaba kānana te āvata sundara ānana dekhe,*
*taba yaha bidhanā krūra karī ghara nayana nimekhe* (191)

When you return from the forest,
we see your beautiful visage.
But then our eyelids blink,
and your lovely vision we fail to see.
Oh, surely , the eyelids are the evidence,
of the creator's utmost cruelty!

फनी फनिन पर अरपे डरपे नाहिन नेक तब ।
छबीली छतीन पर धरत डरत कयों कान्ह मुंवर अब ॥192॥

*phanī phanina para arape ḍarape nāhina neka taba,*
*chabīlī chatīna para dharata ḍarata kyõ kānha kũvara aba* (192)

Unafraid, on the great serpent's hood
you placed your feet and stood![45]
Why then are you afraid, O Kānhā,
to place your feet down
on our beautiful bosoms now?

उपर तुम्हारी कथा अमृत सब ताप सिरावे ।
अमरन अमरा तुच्छ करे ब्रह्मादिक गावे ॥193॥

*ūpara tumhārī kathā amṛta saba tāpa sirāve,*
*amarana amarā tuccha kare brahmādika gāve* (193)

The stories of your deeds
are ambrosia indeed,
one that soothes the burns of all kinds.
Brahmā and the gods thus deride
even the glory of Amarāvatī,[46]
the city where immortals reside!

जानत हों पिय तुम जो डरत ब्रजराज दुलारे ।
कोमल चरण सरोज उरोज कठोर हमारे ॥194॥

*jānata hõ piya tuma jo ḍarata brajarāja dulāre,*
*komala caraṇa saroja uroja kaṭhora hamāre* (194)

O lovely king of Braja, our beloved dear,
we now know what you fear!
Your lotuslike feet are soft and tender,
and our breasts are firmer than ever!

45 Once again, this is a reference to the story of Kāliyā-Mardana.

46 According to the Purāṇic texts, Amarāvatī is a celestial city that is ruled by Indra, the king of gods; everyone who resides in that city have ambrosia to drink and as a result is immortal and eternally young.

सने सने पग धरिये हमको अधिक पियारे ।
कित अटवी में अटत गडत तृणकूर्प अण्यारे ॥195॥

*sane sane paga dhariye hamako adhika piyāre,*
*kita aṭavī mẽ aṭata gaḍata tṛṇakūrpa aṇyāre* (195)

Please, rest your feet slowly down,
as you set them on the ground,
for they are most dear to us!
When you wander far and long,
your feet are hurt and pricked
by the gravel and spine all along.

इति रासक्रीडा वर्णने तृतीयोऽध्याय

|| *iti rāsakrīḍā varṇane tṛtīyo'dhyāyaḥ* ||

So ends, the third chapter describing the play of *rāsa*.

SIX

# Chapter IV: Kṛṣṇa's Solace to the Gopikās

Verses 196–222

यह विधि प्रेम सुधानिध मग्न व्हे करत कलोलें ।
विव्हल व्हे गई बाल लाल सों अलबल बोलें ॥196॥

*yaha vidhi prema sudhānidha magna vhe karata kalolẽ,*
*vivhala vhe gayī bāla lāla sõ alabala bolẽ* (196)

In this way, they play
and meander in the grove,
immersed completely
in the ambrosial treasure of love!
Flurried, flustered, and distraught,
the women then call out to the Lord,
blathering about on and on!

तब तिनही में प्रकट भये नंदनंदनपिय यों ।
दृष्टि बंद कर दुरे बहुर प्रकटे नटवर ज्यों ॥197॥

*taba tinahĩ mẽ prakaṭa bhaye nandananda piya yõ,*
*dṛṣṭi banda kara dure bahura prakaṭe naṭavara jyõ* (197)

And then amidst them, lo and behold,
the beloved son of Nanda emerged!
They shut their eyes and he disappeared;
they opened their eyes and he reappeared!
Just like a skilful conjurer

or the finest of the actors,
he is Naṭavara,[47] the king of performers!

पीतवसन वनमाल धरे मंजुल मुरली हथ ।
मंद मधुर मुस्काय निपट मन्मथ के मन्मथ ॥198॥

*pītavasana vanamāla dhare mañjula muralī hatha,*
*manda madhura musakāya nipaṭa manmatha ke manmatha* (198)

A yellow robe he wore,
with a wildflower garland.
An alluring flute he then held
in his delicate hand!
Sweet and soft smile he smiles,
stirring the heart of the Stirrer of Hearts,
defeating his invincible wiles!

पियहि निरख त्रिय वृन्द उठी सब एक बेर यों ।
फिर आवे घट प्राण बहुर इन्द्री उझकत ज्यों ॥199॥

*piyahi nirakha triya vṛnda uṭhī saba eka bera yõ,*
*phira āve ghaṭa prāṇa bahura indrī ujhakata jyõ* (199)

The group of women then gaze
at their beloved with great intent.
And then they rise up together,
simultaneously in that moment.
As if the breath, the life-giving force,
returns into their bodies.

47 While the word "Naṭavara" literally means the king of performance, Vallabha in his commentary on the song of the flute (Veṇugīta; *Bhāgavata* 10.21) states that Kṛṣṇa is both *naṭa-vapu* and *vara-vapu*. This means that he enjoys the *rasa* of the performance simultaneously as both the performer and as the audience; see *Subodhinī*, edited by Shyam M. Goswami (Kolhapur: Śrīvallabhavidyāpīṭha-Śrīviṭṭhaleśaprabhucaraṇāśrma Trust, 1993), 262-64. This is significant to the essential ontology of Śuddhādvaita because according to Vallabha, akin to the creation of the universe, even this divine dance is Brahman delighting with the reflections of its own self. Thus, he is both the performer and the audience. This point is reiterated by Nandadāsa in verse 244; hence, this ontological dimension of *rāsa* forms the cornerstone of Vallabhite understanding of this episode.

And their senses, aroused by his presence,
liven up, coming out of their quiescence!

महाक्षुधित कों जैसे भोजन सों प्रीत सुनी हे ।
ताही ते सतगुणी सहस्त्र किधों कोटि गुनी हे ॥200॥

*mahakṣudhita kõ jaise bhojana sõ prīta sunī he,*
*tāhī te sataguṇī sahastra kidhõ koṭi guṇī he* (200)

I hear, the one who is starved for good
is madly in love with food.
But a million times more
than a hundred times of that,
they feel their love for him
stronger than they ever had!

कोउ चटपट सों कर लपटी कोउ उरवर लपटी ।
कोउ गरे लपटी कहत भले जु भले कान्हर कपटी ॥201॥

*koū caṭapaṭa sõ kara lapaṭī koū uravara lapaṭī,*
*koū gare lapaṭī kahata bhale ju bhale kānhara kapaṭi* (201)

Some spring forth and hold his hand,
while some proceed to rest
their faces into his chest.
Some embrace him close,
and yet chastise him so.
Well done with your sly endeavour
O Kānhā, you are crafty as ever!

कोउ नागर नग धर की गहि रहि दोउ कर पटकी ।
जानो नव घन ते सटकी दामिनी दामिनी अटकी ॥202॥

*koū nāgara nagadhara kī gahi rahi dou kara paṭaki*
*jāno nava ghana te saṭakī dāminī dāminī aṭakī* (202)

One sublime lady then grabs with both her hands
the ends of the garment worn
by the Bearer of the Mount.
Like the bolts of lightning cling,

with all their thunderous bling,
to the new monsoon cloud.

दोर लपट गई ललित लाले सुख कहत न आवे ।
मीन उछर कें पुलिन परे पुनि पानी पावे ॥203॥

*dora lapaṭa gayī lalita lāle sukha kahat na āve,*
*mīna uchara kẽ pulina pare puni pānī pāve* (203)

One of them runs to embrace her lovely Lord;
her joy cannot be expressed in words.
Like a fish that jumps onto the shore,
and finds its way back to the water, once more!

कोउ पिय भुज गहि लटक रही नव नार नवेली ।
मानो सुंदर श्रंगार विटप लपटी छबि वेली ॥204॥

*koū piya bhuja gahi laṭaka rahī nava nāra navelī,*
*mano sundara śṛṅgāra viṭapa lapaṭī chabi velī* (204)

Then a beauty, with new youthful charms,
holds the hand of her beloved,
and leans on his arms,
as a fine vine of magnificence
encloses a delightful tree of passion.

कोउ कोमल पदकमल कुचन पर राख रही यों ।
परम कृपन धन पाय छाती सों लाय रही ज्यों ॥205॥

*koū komala padakamala kucana para rākha rahī yõ,*
*parama kṛpana dhana pāya chātī sõ lāya rahī jyõ* (205)

Then a lady fair
takes his soft, lotuslike feet
and rests them on bosoms,
with gentle care,
as a great miser who attains wealth
keeps it close to his heart,
never wanting to stay apart.

कोउ पिय रूप नयन भर उर में धर धर आवत ।
मधुर मिष्ट जों वृष्ट दशों दिश अति छबि पावत ।।206।।

*koū piya rūpa nayana bhara ura mẽ dhara dhara āvata,*
*madhura miṣṭa jõ vṛṣṭa daśõ diśa ati chabi pāvata* (206)

One captures his beauty in her eyes,
and preserves it in her heart.
As if sweetness showers all over like rain,
and the ten directions then
appear delightful once again.

कोऊ दशन दिये अधर बिंब गोविंद ही ताडत ।
कोउ एक नयन चकोर चारु मुखचंद निहारत ॥207॥

*koū daśana diye adhara biṁba govinda hi tāḍata,*
*koū eka nayana cakora cāru mukhacanda nihārata* (207)

Another *gopikā* sinks her teeth,
into her lovely lips,
that look like the fruit of *biṁba*,
as she gazes intently at Govinda.
Another stares at his elegant face,
never taking off her eye,
like partridges staring intently
at the moon in the sky.

बैठे पुनि तिहिं पुलिन मांझ आनंद भयो हें ।
छबीली अपनो छालन छबि सों बिछाय दयो हें ॥208॥

*baithe puni tihĩ pulina mā̃jha ānanda bhayo hai,*
*chabīlī apano chālana chabi sõ bichāya dayo hai* (208)

With their hearts full of bliss,
they proceed to sit down then,
on the same shore once again.
The beauties then lay their stoles down,
gracefully spreading them on the ground.

एक एक हरि देव सबे आसन पर वेसे ।
किये मनोरथ पूरन जिनके उपजे जेसे ॥209॥

*eka eka hari deva sabe āsana para vaise,*
*kiye manoratha pūrana jinake upaje jaise* (209)

Each woman then found,
that Hari seated with her alone,
on the garment she laid on the ground.
In this way he fulfilled with brilliance
the desires of their hearts,
and their distinctive preference.

जो अनेक योगेश्वर हिय में ध्यान जु धरही ।
एक ही बेर ही एक मूरत सबनकों सुख विस्तरही ॥210॥

*jo aneka yogeśvara hiya mẽ dhyāna ju dharahī,*
*eka hī bera eka hi mūrata sabana kõ sukha vistarahī* (210)

That which the great yogis
meditate upon with steadfast mind,
it is one, yet at the same time,
blesses each one of them
with timeless bliss sublime!

कहूं कज्जल कहूं कुंकुम कहूं पीकलीक वर ।
जहां राजत नंदनंद कोटि कंदर्प हर ॥211॥

*kahũ kajjala kahũ kuṅkuma kahũ pīkalīka vara,*
*jahā̃ rājata nandananda koṭi kandarpa darpa hara* (211)

With a tint of kohl here, a bit of vermilion there,
and a stain of betel leaf appearing somewhere.
In this way, filled with colour,
wherever the son of Nanda resides,
millions of Kandarpas[48] lose their prides!

48 Another name for the god of love, Kāmadeva.

योगीजन बन जाय यत्न कर कोटि जन्म पचि ।
अति निर्मल कर राखे हिय में आसन रचि रचि ॥212॥

*yogījana bana jāya yatna kara koṭi janma paci,*
*ati nirmala kara rākhe hiye mẽ āsana raci raci* (212)

The yogis dwelling in the forest
strive long and hard for many lives.
And then they carve a pristine resting place
for the supreme Lord in their hearts,
with great care and flawless grace.

कछु छिन तहां नहीं जात नवलनागर सुंदर हरि ।
युवतिन के आसन पर बैठे सुंदर रुचि करि ॥213॥

*kachu china tahā̃ nahī̃ jāta navalanāgara sundara hari,*
*yuvatina ke āsana para baithe sundara ruci kari* (213)

But suave and beautiful Hari,
full of new youthful glory,
refuses to dwell in there,
even for a little while.
And here, the beautiful Lord,
sits joyfully with flair
on the seat laid by the women
with great love and care.

कोटि कोटि ब्रह्मांड यद्यपि इकली ठकुराई ।
ब्रजदेविन की सभा सांवरे अति छबि पाई ॥214॥

*koṭi koṭi brahmāṇḍa yadyapi ikalī ṭhakurāī,*
*braja-devina kī sabhā sā̃vare ati chabi pāī* (214)

Although he reigns supreme
in uncounted universes by himself,
yet the same dark Lord
delights like spring
with the goddesses of Braja alone,
and only in their gathering.

ज्यों नवदल मंडल मध्य कमल कर्णिका भ्राजे ।
यों सब त्रियन के सनमुख सुंदर श्याम बिराजे ॥215॥

*jyõ navadala maṇḍala madhya kamala karṇikā bhrāje,*
*yõ saba triyana ke sanamukha sundara śyāma birāje* (215)

Just as the heart of the lotus manifests
amidst a circle of lotus clusters,
so does the beautiful dark Lord
get seated amidst the women he adored.

बूझन लागी नवलबाल नंदलाल पियहि तब ।
प्रीतरीत की बात मन में मुसकात जात सब ॥216॥

*būjhana lāgī navalabāla nandalāla piyahi taba,*
*prīti rīta ki bāta mana mẽ musakāta jāta saba* (216)

The beautiful women of Braja,
blooming with new youth,
prepare to ask the Son of Nanda.
As they talk about the practice of love,
the traditions and the arts,
they smile bashfully in their hearts.

एक भजते को भजे एक विन भजते भज ही ।
कहो कान्ह ते कवन आहि जो दोहुन त्यजही ॥217॥

*eka bhajate ko bhaje eka vina bhajate bhajahī,*
*kaho kānha te kavana āhi jo dohuna tyajahī* (217)

Some reciprocate the affection
of only those who love them.
Others show affection even to those
who do not love them back.
And then there are some
who abandon both,
even those who love them
and those who love them not.
So, tell me, O Kānhā,
who are you of them all?

यद्यपि जगत गुरु नागर नगधर नंद दुलारे ।
तदपि गोपीन के प्रेम विवस अपने मुख हारे ॥218॥

*yadyapi jagata guru nāgara nagadhara nanda dulāre,*
*tadapi gopīna ke prema vivasa apane mukha hāre* (218)

Although he is the adorable Son of Nanda,
the Bearer of the Mount,
and the mentor of the world,
yet, compelled by the love of the *gopikās*,
he accepts defeat in his own words.[49]

तब बोले ब्रजराज कुंवर हों रिणी तिहारो ।
अपने मन ते दूर करो यह दोष हमारो ॥219॥

*taba bole brajarāja kũvara hõ riṇī tihāro,*
*apane mana te dūra karo yaha doṣa hamāro* (219)

The Lord, the king of Braja, then said,
I am forever in your debt.
So, please do erase this mistake of mine,
from within the depths of your minds.

कोटि कल्प लग तुम प्रति अति उपकार करूं जो ।
हे मन हरणी तरणी अविन अरणी न होऊ तो ॥220॥

*koṭi kalpa laga tuma prati ati upakāra karū̃ jo,*
*he mana haraṇī taraṇī avina araṇī na hoū to* (220)

For millions of eras,
if I will put myself in your service,
O the thieves of my heart,
even if I love you forever,

49 The *Bhāgavata-bhakti* traditions that follow the devotional template of the *gopikās*, commonly advocate this idea that Kṛṣṇa, despite being an all-powerful God, readily accepts defeat at the hands of the women of Braja and their unconditional love. Nandadāsa is highlighting this idea by describing the magnificence of Kṛṣṇa in the second half of verse 218 by stating that regardless of all his powers, he surrenders in front of the *gopikās*. This is a clear reference to *Bhāgavata* 10.32.22, in which Kṛṣṇa declares that he is forever "indebted" to the *gopikās*. This verse marks the triumph of the love of the *gopikās* over the magnificence of the supreme Lord and holds an extremely significance place in the devotional ideal of the Vallabha tradition.

O youthful beauties, yet,
I will never be able to repay your debt!

सकल विश्व आप वस कर मोहि माया सोहत हे ।
प्रेम भई तिहारी माया सो मोहि मोहत हे ॥221॥

*sakala viśva āpa vasa kara mohi māyā sohata hai,*
*prema bhayī tiharī māyā so mohi mohata he* (221)

Māyā, my elusive power,
enchants the entire universe.
But the power of your love is even greater,
for it enchants me, the absolute enchanter!

तुम जो करी सो कोऊ न करे सुन नवल किशोरी ।
लोक वेद की सुद्दढ श्रंखला तृण सम तोरी ॥222॥

*tuma jo karī so koū na kare suna navala kiśorī,*
*loka veda kī sudṛḍha śṛṅkhalā tṛṇa sama torī* (222)

Listen to me,
O youthful beauties!
No one can ever do,
what has been done by you!
You broke away like a mere blade of grass
the strong chain of propriety
set by the Vedas,
and set by the society!

इति रासक्रीडा वर्णने चतुर्थोऽध्याय

|| *iti rāsakrīḍā varṇane caturtho'dhyāyaḥ* ||

So ends the fourth chapter describing the play of *rāsa*.

SEVEN

# Chapter V: Mahārāsa - Culmination of the Ecstatic Dance

Verses 223–286

सुन पिय को रस बचन सबन रीस छांड दयो हे ।
विहसत अपने कंठन लाल लगाय गयो हे ॥223॥

*suna piya ko rasa bacana sabana risa chā̃da dayo hai,*
*vihasata apane kaṇṭhana lāla lagāya layo he* (223)

Their anger melts away as they hear
the ecstatic words of their dear.
Then they embrace their Love,
he who is full of charms.
Smiling with joy,
they enclose him in their arms.

कल्पवृक्ष जड सुनियत वह चिंतत फल दायक ।
वह ब्रजराज कुमार सबे सुखदायक नायक ॥224॥

*kalpavṛkṣa jaḍa suniyata vaha cintata phala dāyaka,*
*vaha brajarāja kumāra sabe sukha-dāyaka nāyaka* (224)

Mighty Kalpavṛkṣa, the wish-fulfilling tree,
is the bestower of all fruits.
But we have heard
that you are truly its roots.
The dearest son of the king of Braja,

O charming young boy,
you are our hero,
the bestower of joy.

कोटि कल्पतरु वसत लसत पद पंकज छाई ।
कामधेनु पुनि कोटि कोटि लोटत रज मांई ॥225॥

*koṭi kalpataru vasata lasata pada paṅkaja chāī,*
*kāmadhenu puni koṭi koṭi loṭata raja mā̃ī* (225)

Millions of Kalpatarus are found[50]
in the shadow of your lotus-feet,
twinkling on the ground.
And millions and millions of Kāmadhenus[51]
roll in the dust of your feet, too.

सो पिय भये अनुकूल तुल्य कोऊ न भये अब ।
निरवध सुख को मूल सूल उनमूल करि सब ॥226॥

*so piya bhaye anukūla tulya koū na bhaye aba,*
*niravadha sukha ko mūla sūla unamūla kari saba* (226)

As the dear Lord became gracious,
no one can equal their status.
Their pain of separation,
that pricked like a spike,
is soothed as they attain him,
he who is the root of all pleasure,
and timeless bliss that lasts forever.

तब आये तेहि सुरतरु तर श्रीगिरिवरधर ।
आरंभत अद्‌त सुरास वह कमल चक्र पर ॥227॥

*taba āye tehi surataru tara śrīgirivaradhara,*
*āraṁbhata adbhuta surāsa vaha kamala cakra para* (227)

50 Kalpavṛkṣa and Kalpataru are synonymous terms, both referring to the celestial wish-fulfilling tree found in Indra's garden.

51 The celestial cow of Indra, traditionally believed to fulfill all wishes.

And then, the splendorous Bearer of the Mount
arrives under the shade of the same ambrosial tree.
On a celestial lotus-disc,
the lovers take the stance,
and then begins
the ecstatic, wondrous dance!

एक काल ब्रजबाल लाल सब चढे जोर कर ।
नमित न इत उत होय सबे नृत्यत विचित्र वर ॥228॥

*eka kāla brajabāla lāla saba caḍhe jora kara,*
*namita na ita uta hoya sabe nṛtyata vicitra vara* (228)

The women of Braja and their beloved
join their hands together and climb
on the divine dancing stage, at the same time!
From one lotus-leaf to another,
gracefully they prance.
Not a single leaf is disarrayed
by the moves of their splendid dance!

पुनि दर्पन सम अवनी रवनी तापर छबि देई ।
बिलुलित कुंडल अलक तिलक झुक झांई लेई ॥229॥

*puni darpaṇa sama avanī ravanī tāpara chabi deī,*
*bilulita kuṇḍala alaka tilaka jhuka jhā̃ī leī* (229)

To add to the beauty,
the floor radiates like a mirror,
on which the ravishing ladies glimmer.
Reflecting off the sparkling mirror,
the adornments on their temples sway;
with dangling earrings and lovely locks,
they swing, move, and dance away!

सबके अंसन धरी सांवरे बांह सुहाई ।
एक हि मूरत लसत लाल आलात की न्याई ॥230॥

*sabake ãnsana dharī sā̃vare bā̃ha suhāī,*
*eka hi mūrata lasata lāla ālāta kī nyāī* (230)

Adorning their beautiful shoulders
is the dark arm of their lover.
Just as a flaming torch that is whirled around
appears like a ring of light,
so does the divine Lord appear,
dancing the round-dance with all his might!

कमल करणिका मध्य जु श्यामा श्याम बनी छबि ।
दोय दोय गोपिन मध्य मोहन लाल बने फ़बि ॥231॥

*kamala karaṇikā madhya ju śyāmā śyāma banī chabi,*
*doya doya gopina madhya mohana lāla bane fabi* (231)

At the centre of the lotus resides
the magnificent dark Lord,
with his lady love by his side!
And amidst every two *gopikās*,
dear Mohana splendidly shines.

मूरत एक अनेक देख अद्‌त शोभा अस ।
मंजुमुकुर मंडल मध्य विधु आन परत जस ॥232॥

*mūrata eka aneka dekha adbhuta śobhā asa,*
*mañjumukura maṇḍala madhya vidhu āna parata jasa* (232)

His one divine form seems to be many,
shimmering around them with wonderful beauty,
as if the moon itself descends
and takes an aesthetic stance
at the centre of the majestic mirror,
the wonderful circular stage of dance.

सकल त्रियन के मध्य सांवरो प्रिय शोभित अस ।
रत्नावली मध्य नीलमणि अद्‌त झलके जस ॥233॥

*sakala triyana ke madhya sā̃varo priya śobhita asa,*
*ratnāvalī madhya nīlamaṇi adbhuta jhalake jasa* (233)

In the middle of beautiful ladies,
the exquisite dark Lord appears so.
As if in the midst of the jewel of every kind,
a blue sapphire dazzles the mind!

नव मरकत मणि श्याम कनक मणि गण ब्रजबाला ।
श्रीवृन्दावन को रीझ मानो पहराई माला ॥234॥

*nava marakata maṇi śyāma kanaka maṇi gaṇa brajabālā,*
*śrī-vṛndāvana ko rījha māno paharāī mālā* (234)

The dark lord, beaming like a Markata jewel,[52]
and the golden gleam of the Braja women,
together, they appear like a grand necklace,
displayed on the splendorous Vṛndāvana,
with exquisite elegance!

बाजत नूपुर किंकिणी करतल मंजुल मुरली
ताल मृदंग उपंग सबे एक सवर जुरली ॥235॥

*bājata nūpura kiṅkiṇī karatala mañjula muralī,*
*tāla mṛdaṅga upaṅga sabe eke svara juralī* (235)

Their anklets jingle and bracelets tinkle,
as they clap their hands at the tune,
along with the sweet sound of the flute!
The beat of the mṛdaṅga[53]
and rhythmic instruments of all kinds
attune themselves together
to produce a melody divine.

मृदुल मुरज टंकार तार झंकार मिली ध्वनि ।
मधुर यंत्र की तार भ्रमर गुंजार मिली पुनि ॥235॥

52 Markatamaṇi is a divine jewel, usually emerald in hue, and is believed to be studded in the crown of Lord Viṣṇu.

53 Mṛdaṅgam is a percussion instrument of ancient origin, made out of clay, and is today typically used in Carnatic Classical Music. Its later descendant is the more popular Pakhāvaj, a similar shaped, two-headed wooden drum well-known in Hindustani Classical Music.

*mṛdula muraja ṭaṅkāra tāra jhaṅkāra milī dhvani,*
*madhura yantra kī tāra bhramara guñjāra milī puni* (236)

The soft sound of the Muraja drums
mingles with the sweet strums!
Adding to the tuneful tones,
the bees buzz, hum, and sing,
blending with the melodic instruments,
and their harmonious strings!

तेसी मृदु पर पटकन चटकन कठतारन की ।
लठकन मटकन चटकन कंकण कुंडल हारन की ॥237॥

*tesi mṛdu pada paṭakana caṭakana kaṭhatārana kī,*
*laṭakana maṭakana caṭakana kaṅkaṇa kuṇḍala hārana kī* (237)

The sweet tapping of their feet,
and the clicking of claves on the beat![54]
As they swirl, whirl, and swing,
their bangles, earrings, and necklaces
clash, chime, and ring.
Their grace, their poise, and their countenance
all come together when they move with elegance.

सांवरे पिय संग नृत्यत चंचल ब्रज की बाला ।
जनु घन मंजुल मंडल खेलत दामिनी माला ॥238॥

*sā̃vare piya saṅga nṛtyata cañcala braja ki bālā,*
*janu ghana mañjula maṇḍala khelata dāmini mālā* (238)

The zestful women of Braja,
full of amorous fervour,
dance with their dark lover
as if a lovely dark cloud
made a circle on the ground,

54 "Claves" is my translation of Kaṭhatāra, which is a similar-sounding ancient folk music instrument that is made out of wood and appears like a pair of sticks.

and a wreath of lightning plays within,
by going round and round!

छबीली त्रियन के पाछें आछें बिलुलित वेणी ।
चंचल रूप लतन संग डोलत जनु अलिश्रेणी ॥239॥

*chabīlī triyana ke pāchẽ āchẽ bilulita veṇī,*
*cañcala rūpa latana saṅga ḍolata janu aliśreṇī* (239)

As the pretty girls twirl on the rhythm,
their lovely braids flow along with them
as if a swarm of bees follow in line,
after a beautiful, bouncy vine!

मोहन पिय की मलकन ढलकन मोर मुकुट की ।
सदा बसों मन मेरे फरकन पियरे पटकी ॥240॥

*mohana piya kī malakana ḍhalakana mora mukuṭa kī,*
*sadā basõ mana mere pharakana piyare paṭakī* (240)

The peacock feather on dear Mohana's crown
sways with grace, swinging up and down!
In my heart will always reside
the flapping of my beloved's robe,
and the delightful way it glides!

वदन कमल पर अलक छुरित कछु श्रमकण झलकन ।
सदा रहो मन मेरे मोर मुकुट की ढलकन ॥241॥

*vadana kamala para alaka churita kachu śramakaṇa jhalakana,*
*sada raho mana mere mora-mukuṭa ki ḍhalakana* (241)

His lovely locks dance along,
and the droplets of sweat shine
on his lotus-like body divine!
Oh, dwell in my heart always,
the peacock-crown and its pleasant sways!

कोउ सखि कर पर तिरप बांध नृत्यत छबीली त्रिय ।
मानो करतल लटू करत देख लटू होत पिय ॥242॥

*koū sakhi kara para tirapa bā̃dha nṛtyata chabīlī triya,*
*māno kartala laṭū karata dekha laṭū hota piya* (242)

Taking his hand in her hand,
a beautiful girl, swirls and twirls.
She dances by tapping her feet,
thrice on every beat.
Like a spinning top, that whirls atop,
on the beloved's hand.
Smitten and besotted,
he watches her moves grand!

कोऊ नायक के भेद भाव लावन्य रूप वस ।
अभिनय कर दिखरावत गावत गुण पिय के अस ॥243॥

*koū nāyaka ke bheda bhāva lāvanya rūpa vasa,*
*abhinaya kara dikharāvata gāvata guṇa piya ke asa* (243)

One amongst them, is spellbound,
by her beloved's lovely form.
And so she reveals all the mysteries,
of her lover's beguiling charm!
She acts, enacts, and imitates,
his enticing, alluring ways,
and then sings the praise,
of her beloved's lovely traits!

तब नागर नंदलाल चाहत चित चकित भये यों ।
निज प्रतिबिंब विलास निरख शिशु भूल रहत ज्यों ॥244॥

*taba nāgara nandalāla cāhata cita cakita bhaye yõ,*
*nija pratibiṁba vilāsa nirakha śiśu bhūla rahata jyõ* (244)

Endeared by the dance, the suave son of Nanda,
is filled with joy and wonder!
Like a child who forgets the world,
when he sees himself in the mirror.

In the same way, does the Lord delight,
with the reflections of his own light.

रीझ परस्पर वारत अंबर आभरण अंग के ॥
अवर तहीं वन रहत तहां अद्‌त रंग रंग के ।।245॥

*rījha parspara vārata aṁbara ābharaṇa aṅga ke,*
*avara tahī̃ vana rahata tahā̃ adbhuta raṅga raṅga ke* (245)

Pleased with each other, they celebrate by presenting,
the garments and jewellery that adorned their body.[55]
But in that very moment,
the parts of the body that are left bare
are clothed and bedecked again,
by wonderful ornaments and colourful wears!

कोऊ मुरली संग जुरली रंगीली रसहि बढावत ।
कोऊ मुरली कों छेक छबीली अद्‌त गावत ॥246॥

*koū muralī saṅga juralī raṅgīlī rasahi baḍhāvata,*
*koū muralī kõ cheka chabīlī adbhuta gāvata* (246)

One syncs her voice with the flute,
enhancing the ecstatic colourful tune!
Another pierces the sound of the flute,
as she beautifully croons,
hitting the higher notes of the tune.

ताहि सांवरो कुंवर रीझ हँस लेत भुजन भर ।
चुंबन कर मुख सदन वदन ते दे तम्बोल ढर ॥247॥

55 The word vārata in the main verse indicates a traditional way of showing appreciation wherein one typically waves a valuable piece of item in front of the person who is being appreciated and then that item is given away as donation. This typically done after a rendition of any kind of performing arts, especially after something extraordinary has been presented such as an excellent move in a dance or a particularly difficult vocalisation or simply, to appreciate the beauty and elegance of the person in that moment. This act denotes that one single moment of that performance was more precious than the most precious item that one owns.

Similarly, in this verse, it is shown that as they were dancing in the forest where they did not have any valuables to give away with them and so, they started giving away the clothes and jewellery that they wore to celebrate each other's performance.

*tāhi sā̃varo kũvara rījha hā̃sa leta bhujana bhara,*
*cuṁbana kara mukha sadana vadana te de tambola ḍhara* (247)

Pleased by her song and laughing delightfully,
the dark young Lord, embraces her tightly.
With a tender kiss, he offers in her mouth,
an ecstatic piece of betel leaf,
to satiate her drouth.

जग में जो संगीत रीत सुर मुनि रिझवत जिहिं ।
सो ब्रज त्रियन के सनेह जु गमन आगम गावत तिहिं ॥248॥

*jaga mẽ jo saṅgīta rīta sura muni rijhavata jihĩ,*
*so braja triyana ke saneha ju gamana āgama gāvata tihĩ* (248)

The music, dance, and the songs,
that pleases the world alike,
be it be men, sages, gods, and the like.
But when Braja women sing with love
that exotic music, divine and mystifying,
simply comes to them, without even trying.

जो ब्रजदेवी निर्तत मंडल रास महा छबि ।
सो रस केसे वरण सके यहां एसो को कबि ॥249॥

*jo brajadevī nirtata maṇḍala rāsa mahā chabi,*
*so rasa kese varaṇa sake yahā̃ aiso ko kabi* (249)

The goddesses of Braja look sublime,
as they dance the round-dance,
on a circular stage divine!
Is there poet in the whole world,
who can describe this ecstasy with his words?

राग रागिनी समझन कों जो बोलवो सुहायो ।
सो कापे कहि आवे जो ब्रजदेविन गायो ॥250॥

*rāga rāginī samajhana kõ jo bolavo suhāyo,*
*so kāpe kahi āve jo brajadevina gāyo* (250)

Even their ordinary speech,
resembles the rāgas and the rāginīs.[56]
Who can describe then,
the songs sung by these Braja women?

पिय ग्रीव भुज मेल केलि कमनीय बढी अति ।
लटक लटक के निर्तत कापे कहि आवे गति ॥251॥

*piya grīva bhuja mela keli kamanīya baḍhī ati,*
*laṭaka laṭaka ke nirtata kāpe kahi āve gati* (251)

As they put their arms around their lover,
amorous playful love fills them over!
And so, they dance with a romantic grace,
who can ever describe their exotic pace?

छबि सों निर्तत मटकन लटकन मंडल डोलत ।
कोटि अमृत सम मुसकन मंजुल ताथेई बोलत ॥252॥

*chabi sõ nirtata maṭakana laṭakana maṇḍala ḍolata,*
*koṭi amṛta sama musakana mañjula tātheī bolata* (252)

As they dance, posing with finesse,
the stage itself moves,
along with their artistic moves!
Millions of ambrosias are contained,
in their beautiful smile.
And tātheī, tātheī,[57] they repeat,
dancing on every beat!

56 Rāga is a pattern of melodic mode in Indian classical music, consisting at least of five notes. Rāgas form the fundamental basis of musical tradition in India, and each rāgas has its own characteristic and emotivity. Rāginī, is a feminine counterpart of a rāga, which is typically used to further refine the rāgas and give them additional attributes, patterns, and embellishments. A rāga may be associated with one or more rāginī, for instance, in the fifteenth-century text Saṅgīta-Darpaṇa, Dāmdodara Miśrā describes six rāgas with thirty rāginīs creating a musical system enriched with thirty-six patterns.

57 Tātheī is an exclamation used in classical dances to denote the beats of the rhythm.

कोऊ उनते अति गावत सुलप ले नई नई ।
सब संगीत जु छेकें सुंदर गान करत भई ॥253॥

*koū unate ati gāvata sulapa le naī naī,*
*saba saṅgīta ju chekẽ sundara gāna karata bhayī* (253)

One of them renders ālāpa[58] of every kind,
creating a new one every time.
All kinds of music in the world,
fades in front of her voice,
as she proceeds to render,
a song full of splendour!

आप आपनी गति भेद तहां नृत्य करत तब ।
गंधर्व मोहे तिहि क्षण सुंदर गान करत जब ॥254॥

*āpa āpanī gati bheda tahā̃ nṛtya karata taba,*
*gandharva mohe tihi kṣaṇa sundara gāna karata jaba* (254)

They dance with their unique gaits,
displaying their artistic traits.
Even Gandharvas, the celestial musicians,
are besotted by their poise,
when they render a lovely melody,
in their tuneful voice.

भुज डंडन सों मिलत ललित मंडल निर्तत छबि ।
कुंडल कुच सों उरझे मरझ रहे तहां बडरे कबि ॥255॥

*bhuja ḍaṇḍana sõ milata lalita maṇḍala nirtata chabi,*
*kuṇḍala kuca sõ urajhe murajha rahe tahā̃ baḍare kabi* (255)

58 Ālāpa is a kind of vocalisation that forms the opening section of a performance and is rendered unmetered, improvised, and unaccompanied by any instrument except the supporting instrument Tānpurā, which only provides a continuous harmonic drone. Ālāpa invokes the listeners to the absorb the essence of the song and sets the mood and rasa of the composition. Although impromptu to an extent, it is still defined by a few sets of rules and has multiple variations in singing styles. Nandadāsa is suggesting here that the ālāpa of the gopikās was absolutely unique and did not resemble any popular styles to underline the mastery of these cowherd girls over intricacies of classical music. It is a recurring theme in the Bhāgavata-bhakti traditions that the gopikās only appear to be simple village belles, but are well-versed in both the arcane knowldeg of the vedic scriptures and fineries of arts and music.

Linking arms together,
they hit their sticks on the rhythm.[59]
And they so dance on the circular stage,
forming a ravishing vision!
When they swirl and whirl with vigour,
their earrings entangle with their breasts.
The greatest of poets are left speechless,
at the sight of their passionate zest!

पिय के मुकुट की लटकन मुरली नाद भई अस ।
कुहक कुहक यों बाजत मंजुल मोर भरे रस ॥256॥

*piya ke mukuṭa kī laṭakana muralī nāda bhayī asa,*
*kuhaka kuhaka yõ bājata mañjula mora bhare rasa* (256)

The glimmer of the beloved's crown,
and his flute making an alluring sound!
As if kuhu-kuhu, says a peacock,
in his beautiful voice,
filled with ecstatic joys!

सिर ते कुसुमन सुंदर वरषत अति आनंद भर ।
जनु पद गति पर रीझ अलक पूजन फूलन कर ॥257॥

*sira te kusumana sundara varaṣata ati ānanda bhara,*
*janu pada gati para rījha alaka pūjana phūlana kara* (257)

Beautiful blooms braided in their hair,
come falling down with great delight,
showering everywhere.
It seems as if, the blooms in their tresses,
are pleased by their moves,
and offer themselves on the street,
to worship their delicate feet.

59 This is the translation of the original term "ḍanḍana," which I believe refers to *dāndiyā*, a kind of round-dance that operates in pairs. Traditionally the group contains an even number of people, and each person hits their sticks (*dāndiyās*) with their partners' and moves clockwise in a circle.

श्रमजल बिंदु सुंदर रंग भर कहूं कहूं बरषत ।
प्रेम भक्त विरला जिनके जिनके हिय सरसत ॥258॥

*śramajala bindu sundara raṅga bhara kahū̃ kahū̃ barasata,*
*prema bhakta viralā jinake tinake hiya sarasata* (258)

Droplets of sweat full of colour
shower here and there.
Only the loving devotees,
who are rarest of the rare,
have their hearts soaked
in this nectareous fare.

श्रीवृंदावन को त्रिविध पवन व्यजना सो बिलोलें ।
जहां जहां श्रम अवलोकत तहां तहां रस भर डोलें ॥259॥

*śrīvṛndāvana trividha pavana vyajanā so bilolẽ,*
*jahā̃ jahā̃ śrama avalokata tahā̃ tahā̃ rasa bhara dolẽ* (259)

An ethereal breeze, with three attributes sublime,[60]
fans the splendorous Vṛndāvana at all times!
Wherever it spots, a little weariness,
there it flows, filled with ecstasy,
refreshing with its pleasant gentleness!

उडु नव अरुन अबीर अद्‌त शशि मंडल ऐसे ।
प्रेम जाल के गोलक कछु छबि उपजत जैसे ॥260॥

*uḍu nava aruna abīra adbhuta śaśi maṇḍala aise,*
*prema jāla ke golaka kachu chabi upajata jaise* (260)

A prismatic disk forms in the sky,
as the stars glimmer with a carmine hue,
and the moon glows with its celestial crew!
Like a stellar mesh forming into the ether,
with starry halos that glisten all over.

60 *Trividha pavana*, that is, "breeze with three divine attributes," is a common phrase found in the *aṣṭa-chāpa* compositions. Although there is no source to conclusively state what these three attributes are, the general idea is that it refers to the triad of coolness (*śitalatā*), softness (*mandatva*), and fragrance (*sugandhva*), which collectively make a breeze aesthetically favourable.

कुसुम धूंधरि कुंज मत्त मधुकर निवेश तहां ।
ऐसे हुलसत आवत ग्रीवन लटक केस तहां ॥261॥

*kusuma dhūdhari kuñja matta madhukara niveśa tahā̃,*
*aise hulasata āvata grīvana laṭaka kesa tahā̃* (261)

Flowering blooms spread their pollen,
forming a misty arbour.
Intoxicated by its nectar,
honeybees swarm all over.
Lovely locks of Braja women
dangle around their necks.
Like a line of bumble bees,
buzzing about with glee!

नव पल्लव की श्रेणी अति सुख देनी दरसे ।
सुंदर सुमन सुनि रखत अति आनंदहि बरसे ॥262॥

*nava pallava kī śreṇi ati sukha denī darase,*
*sundara sumana suni rakhata ati ānandahi barase* (262)

New buds blossom in a delicate sequence,
spreading great joy simply by their presence.
In them bloom beautiful flowers,
pouring boundless bliss in the bowers.

पवन थक्यो शशि थक्यो थक्यो उडु मंडल सगरो ।
पाछें रवि रथ थक्यों चल्यो नहिं आगे डगरो ॥263॥

*pavana thakyo śaṣi thakyo thakyo uḍu maṇḍala sagaro,*
*pachẽ ravi ratha thakyo calyo nahī̃ āge ḍagaro* (263)

The breeze ceases to blow and the moon stupefied,
and so are the stars transfixed in the sky!
Even the chariot of the sun is amazed,
and halts in its path to gaze!

विहरत रति अविरूद्ध युद्ध सुरत रससागर ।
उज्वल प्रेम उजागर नागर सब गुण आगर ॥264॥

*viharata rati aviruddha yuddha surata rasasāgara,*
*ujjvala prema ujāgara nāgara saba guṇa āgara* (264)

Unstoppable in the battle of love,
they immerse in the nectareous sea,
filled with pure ecstasy!
And then comes to the fore
their pristine love for the Lord,
who is the abode of all attributes pure!

हार हार में उरझ उरझ बहियां में बहियां ।
नील पीत पट उरझ उरझ नथ वेसर महियां ॥265॥

*hāra hāra mẽ urajha urajha bahiyā̃ me bahiyā̃,*
*nīla pīta paṭa urajha urajha natha vesara mahiyā̃* (265)

Their necklaces intertwine,
and their arms link together.
Nose rings entangle with the nose studs,
and the yellow garments with the blue[61]
as the night passes through!

श्रम भरे सुंदर अंग सरस अति मिलत ललित गति ।
अंसन पर भुज दिये लटक शोभा शोभित अति ॥266॥

*śrama bhare sundara aṅga sarasa ati milata lalita gati,*
*ansana para bhuja diye laṭaka śobhā śobhita ati* (266)

Their beautiful bodies,
covered in the droplets of sweat,
meet with pure ecstasy,
as they skilfully gyrate.
The beauty of their arms is enhanced,

61 In the compositions of the *aṣṭa-chāpa*, there is a common phrase of description, namely, *nilāṁbara pītāṁbara kī chavi*, which means the vision of the "blue robe" contrasting the "yellow robe." It is typically used to describe that Kṛṣṇa wears a yellow robe (*pītāṁbara*) on his blue body, while his consort Rādhā or the *gopikās* wear blue garments (*nilāṁbara*) on their golden bodies. Thus, they are portrayed to be wearing the colour of each other's texture of skin, signifying their mutual devotion.

as they elegantly dangle
on each other's dainty shoulders!

टूटी मुक्ता माल छूटि रही सांवरे उर पर ।
मानो गिरि ते सुरसुरी द्वै विधि धार धसी धर ॥267॥

*ṭūṭī muktā māla chūti rahī sā̃vare ura para,*
*māno giri te surasurī dve vidhi dhāra dhasī dhara* (267)

Pearls from the broken necklace
fall on the dark Lord's chest
as if from both sides of a mountain
Ganges comes rushing down
and gushes into the ground!

अद्‌त रस रह्यो रास रस गीत ध्वनि सुन मोहे मुनि ।
सिला सलिल व्हे चली सलिल व्हे रही सिला पुनि ॥268॥

*adbhuta rasa rahyo rāsa gīta dhvani suna mohe muni,*
*silā salila vhe calī salila vhe rahī silā puni* (268)

So wonderful is the ecstasy of the round dance
that the sound of its songs bewitches
even the most austere of the sages!
The stones are turned into streams, and
the running streams are turned to stones again!

रीझ शरद की रजनी न जनी किति एक बाढी ।
विलसत सजनी श्याम यथा रुचि अति रति गाढी ॥269॥

*rījha śarada kī rajanī na janī kiti eka bāḍhī,*
*vilasata sajanī śyāma yathā ruci ati rati gāḍhi* (269)

So pleased is the lovely autumn night
that it prolongs its stay and stops in time.
And so the dark Lord
relishes with his darlings,
for, as the night lengthens,
his love too begins to deepen!

यह विधि विविध विलास विलस सुख कुंज सदन के ।
चले यमुना जल क्रीडन ब्रीडन कोटि मदन के ॥270॥

*yaha vidhi vividha vilāsa vilasa sukha kuñja sadana ke,*
*cale yamunā jala krīḍana brīḍana koṭi madana ke* (270)

In this way they savour the joys of all kind
in their lovely grove, the pleasure palace divine!
To play in the waters of Yamunā,
when they came,
millions of Madanas[62]
are put to shame!

उरसी मरगजीमाल चाल मत्त गज गति मलकत ।
घूमत रस भरे नयन गंडस्थल श्रमकण झलकत ॥271॥

*urasī maragajīmāla cāla matta gaja gati malakata,*
*ghūmata rasa bhare nayana gaṇḍasthala śramakaṇa jhalakata* (271)

When he walks with a regal gait,
like that of a euphoric tusker,
the garland that he wears,
though crumpled, wilted, and pressed,
swings majestically on his chest!
His eyes, full of ecstasy,
rove, spin, and rotate,
while his curvy cheeks glisten
with pearly beads of sweat!

धाय यमुना जल लसे लसे छबि परत न वरणी ।
विहरत जनु गजराज संग लिये तरणी करणी ॥272॥

*dhāya yamunā jala lase lase chabi parata na varaṇī,*
*viharata janu gajarāja saṅga liye taraṇī karaṇī* (272)

Into the lovely waters of Yamunā
they plunge and dive

62 Another name for the god of love, Kāmadeva.

Oh, the beauty of it,
who can ever describe?
Like the king of the elephants plays,
along with his ravishing mates!

त्रियन तन झलमलत वदन तहां अति छबि पाये ।
फूल रहे जनु यमुना कनक के कमल सुहाये ॥273॥

*triyana tana jhalamalata vadana tahā̃ ati chabi pāye,*
*phūla rahe janu yamunā kanaka ke kamala suhāye* (273)

The beautiful bodies of the women
look exquisite then,
shimmering amidst the brook,
as they gracefully swim in!
In the pleasing waters of Yamunā it seems,
golden lotuses blossom with beauty,
appearing divinely pretty!

मंजुल अंजली भर भर पिय के तिय जल मेलत ।
जानो अली अरविंद वृंद मकरंद हि खेलत ॥274॥

*mañjula añjalī bhara bhara piya ke tiya jala melata,*
*jāno alī aravinda vṛnda makaranda hi khelata* (274)

Filling their delicate palms with water,
they sprinkle on the beloved lover.
And so he appears, like a black bee
playing with sweet nectar,
sprayed by lotuses together![63]

छिरकत छल सों छेल जो मंजुल अंजली भर भर ।
अरुण कमल मंडली फाग खेलत जनु रंग कर ॥275॥

*chirakata chala sõ chela jo mañjula añjalī bhara bhara,*
*aruṇa kamala maṇḍalī phāga khelata janu raṅga kara* (275)

63 In this metaphor, Kṛṣṇa is compared with the bumblebee due to his dark form, the water sprinkled by the *gopikās* is analogous to the spout of the nectar, and the hands of the *gopikās* are to the lotuses.

The handsome Lord
then employed his guile;
filling his lovely palms with water,
he drenched them in style!
As if a group of red lotuses
gather in glee,
and with colours of all kinds,
they play Holī![64]

रुचिर दृगंचल चंचल अंचल वर जगमग अस ।
सरस कनक के कंजन खंजन जाल परत जस ॥276॥

*rucira dṛgañcala cañcala añcala vara jagamaga asa,*
*sarasa kanaka ke kañjana khañjana jāla parata jasa* (276)

The hems of their pretty eyelids
are restlessly twinkling!
As if little songbirds are ensnared
amidst the golden lotuses,
which are filled with ecstasies![65]

यमुना जल में दुर मुर कामिनि करत कलोलें ।
मानो नवघन भीतर दामिनी दामिनी डोलें ॥277॥

*yamunā jala mẽ dura mura kāmini karata kalolẽ,*
*māno navaghana bhītara dāminī daminī dolẽ* (277)

Ravishing women splash back and forth
in the water of Yamunā, full of mirth!
As if lightning bolts saunter with joy
amidst the new rainclouds in the sky!

64 Akin to the previous verse, "red lotus" is a reference to their hands which are reddened by *mahāvar*, a kind of red dye that was originally made using lac. *Mahāvar* is applied as kind of ornamentation to beautify hands and feet and is used in India even today, mainly by brides of some regions and by classical dancers.

65 "Songbird" is my translation for *khañjana*, which is name of a kind of Indian wagtail (also a songbird), that is traditionally used as a metaphor for beautiful and restless eyes.

कमलन त्यज अलिगण मुखकमलन ढिंग जब आवत ।
छबिसों छबीलो छेल भेट तिन छिनहीं उडावत ॥278॥

*kamalana tyaja aligaṇa mukha-kamalana ḍhiṅga jaba āvata,*
*chabi sõ chabīlo chela bheṭa tina chinahī̃ uḍāvata* (278)

Near the lotuslike faces of pretty women,
the covetous bees tend to arrive,
and the cluster of real lotuses are left behind!
At that very moment, the gallant Lord,
gracefully embraces them and adores,
so as to shoo the bees away,
and allay his beloved's dismay!

कबहुंक मिली सब बाल लाल छिरकत छबि सों अस ।
मनसिज पायो राज आज अभिषेक होत जस ॥279॥

*kabahũka milī saba bāla lāla chirakata chabi sõ asa,*
*manasija pāyo rāja āja abhiṣekha hota jasa* (279)

Sometimes the women gather around,
surrounding the young Lord from everywhere,
and sprinkle water on him with artistic flair!
As if today the god of love is coronated
and is then ceremoniously anointed!

तिनकी सुंदर कांति भांत मनमोहन भावे ।
बाल वेष छबि पैहें कछु हूं कहत न आवे ॥280॥

*tinakī sundara kānti bhā̃ta manamohana bhāve,*
*bāla veṣa chabi paihẽ kachu hū̃ kahata na āve* (280)

The charmer of hearts, the divine Lord,
is charmed by the splendour
of their majestic manners and glorious grandeur!
The beauty of these women, the way they dress,
who can describe their inexpressible finesse?

भीज वसन तन लपटे अद्‌त छबि कहा कहिये ।
नयनन को नहीं बेन बेन को नयन नहींये ॥281॥

*bhīja vasana tana lapaṭe adbhuta chabi kahā kahiye,*
*nayanana ko nahī̃ bena bena ko nayana nahī̃ye* (281)

When the wet garments stick stunningly to their curves,
their magnificence cannot be expressed in words!
Both are inadequate like so,
As the tongue does not have the eyes,
and the eyes do not possess a tongue,
so how can their glory ever be sung?

चीर निचोवत युवती नीर देख भई अधीर मन ।
तन बिछुरन की पीर चीर रोवत अँसुवन जन ॥282॥

*cīra nicovata yuvatī nīra dekha bhayī adhīra mana,*
*tana bichurana kī pīra cīra rovata ãsuvana jana* (282)

As the young women squeeze their clothes dry,
their minds grow restless, and they begin to feel shy!
Even their garments feel the pain
of parting from the bodies of Braja women.
It appears as if they have begun to cry
and water that is squeezed out
are their tears flowing by!

तब एक द्रुम तन चितये कुंवर वर आज्ञा दीनी ।
निरमल अंबर भूषण तिनहीं वरषा कीनी ॥283॥

*taba eka druma tana citaye kũvara vara ājñā dīnī,*
*niramala aṁbara bhūṣaṇa tinahī̃ varaṣā kīnī* (283)

And then the young Lord
looks at a branch of a tree;
to allay their fears,
he gestures it thus.
And so the tree lavishly bestows
glamorous jewelleries and pristine robes!

अपनी अपनी रुचिके पहरे वसन बने तब ।
जग में जे मोहन आये तिनकी मोहनी सब ॥284॥

*apanī apanī rucike pahare vasana bane taba,*
*jaga mẽ je mohana āye tinakī mohanī saba* (284)

Then each one of them wear
the clothes they most desire,
and divinely gorgeous they look,
in their ethereal attire!
One who came to enchant the world,
the absolute enchanter,[66]
they look like his enticing spells,
like the charms of the divine charmer!

यह शरद की जितयेक परम मनोहर राती ।
खेलत रास रसिक पिय प्रतिक्षण नई नई भांती ॥285॥

*yaha śarada kī jitayeka parama manohara rātī,*
*khelata rāsa rasika piya pratikṣaṇa naī naī bhā̃tī* (285)

On all of these delightful nights
of this wonderful autumn bright,
The ecstatic Lord performed
the great play of Rāsa,
with a new style of every kind,
in each moment of its time!

ब्रह्म मुहूरत कुंवर कान्ह सब घर आये जब ।
गोपन अपनी गोपी अपने ढिंग मानी तब ।।286॥

*brāhma muhūrata kũvara kānha saba ghara āye jaba,*
*gopana apanī gopī apane ḍhiṅga mānī taba* (286)

Young Kānhā and they all
then come back home,
at the very break of dawn!
Thinking their women were home all night,
the cowherd men revel in delusion,
for they are enchanted by Māyā,
the supreme Lord's divine illusion!

66 This is a reference to Kṛṣṇa.

इति रासक्रीडा वर्णने पञ्चमोऽध्यायः

|| *iti rāsakrīḍā varṇane pañcamo'dhyāyaḥ* ||

So ends the fifth chapter describing the play of *rāsa*.

EIGHT

# *Phala-Śruti*: Significance of the *Mahārāsa*

Verses 287–301

नित्य रास रस मत्त नित्य श्रीगोपीजन वल्लभ ।
नित्य निगम जो कहियत नित्य नौतन अति दुर्लभ ॥287॥

*nitya rāsa rasa matta nitya śrīgopījana vallabha,*
*nitya nigama jo kahiyata nitya nautana ati durlabha* (287)

Eternal is the ecstasy of this dance,
as the splendorous beloved of the *gopikās*
revels endlessly in its trance!
Forever it seems anew,
changing its divine hue;
it is rare, exotic, and recherché.
The Vedas sing its glories every day!

यह अद्‌त रस रास कहत कछु न आवे ।
शेष सहस्त्र मुख गावत अजहूं पार न पावे ॥288॥

*yaha adbhuta rasa rāsa kahata kachu na āve,*
*śeṣa sahastra mukha gāvata ajahũ pāra na pāve* (288)

The ecstasy of this wondrous dance divine,
it can never ever be described!
It could not be sung
even by the great serpent Śeṣa,
who has but a thousand tongues!

शिव मनही मन धावे काहू नहिं जनावे ।
सनक सनंदन नारद सारद अति मन भावे ॥289॥

*śiva manahī mana dhāve kāhū nahī janāve,*
*sanaka sanandana nārada sārada ati mana bhāve* (289)

Śiva meditates on it,
over and over again,
but he still abstains
from telling anyone of this tale.
It pleases the hearts of all
the spiritual sons of Brahmā[67]
or the sage of the gods[68]
Even the Goddess of Speech herself[69]
is delighted by its spell!

यद्यपि यह पद कमला अमला सेवित निशि दिन ।
यह रस अपने सपने कबहूं नाहिन पायो तिन ॥290॥

*yadyapi yaha pada kamalā amalā sevita nisi dina,*
*yaha rasa apane sapane kabahũ nāhina pāyo tina* (290)

Although the lotus-born Goddess
serves the supreme Lord
and worships his divine feet,
every day indeed!
Yet, she never attains,
this divine ecstasy by any means,
not even in her dreams![70]

67 These are Sanaka, Sanandana, Sanātana, and Sanatkumāra, the first mind-born sons of Brahmā, who collectively took the vow of lifelong celibacy. They are considered to be the greatest of the enlighten beings and among of the foremost devotees of Lord Viṣṇu. Blessed with eternal youth, they always travel together and so are always referenced together in the texts.

68 Nārada

69 Goddess Sarasvatī

70 The tales associated with the Braja Vaiṣṇava tradition place Lakṣmī secondary to the *gopikās*, as she arrogantly believes that the supreme Lord belongs only to her. This is often contrasted with the unconditional love of the Yamunā and the *gopikās*, who share the Lord with other devotees and invite them to participate in the celebration of divine love. Hence, Lakṣmī does not gain the right to enter this divine dance, as it is stated in the lore of Bel-ban (one of the

अज अजहू रज वांछत सुंदर वृंदावन की ।
सोऊ तनक न पावत शूल मिटत नहीं मन की ॥291॥

*aja ajahū raja vā̃chata sundara vṛndavana kī,*
*soū tanaka na pāvata śūla miṭata nahī̃ mana kī* (291)

The eternal unborn gods forever lust
for the exotic Vṛndāvana's divine dust!
But their hearts are stung by searing spike
when they fail to attain
even a single divine grain!

बिन अधिकारी भये नहीं श्रीवृंदावन सूझे ।
रेन कहां ते सूझे जब लगि वस्तु न बूझे ॥292॥

*bina adhikārī bhaye nahī̃ śrīvṛndāvana sūjhe,*
*rena kahā̃ te sūjhe jaba laga vastu na būjhe* (292)

Those who do not belong here
are unable to see
the splendorous Vṛndāvana,
and its divine ecstasy!
For how would they ever perceive,
if they fail to see the supreme essence?
And so, they dwell forever
in the perpetual darkness of ignorance!

निपट निकट घट पट में जों अंतरयामी आही ।
विषय विदूषित इन्द्रिय पकर सकत नहीं ताही ॥293॥

*nipaṭa nikaṭa ghaṭa ghaṭa mẽ jõ antarayāmī āhī,*
*viṣaya vidūṣita indriya pakara sakata nahī̃ tāhī* (293)

He, the supreme Lord, is here,
always very near,
residing as the inner controller
of every aspect of the sphere!
But the sense organs that are blemished

principal twelve forests of Braja). See David, L. Haberman, *Acting as a Way of Salvation* (New York: Oxford University Press, 2001), 87.

by wallowing in worldly pleasures
can never grasp his pure Being,
for it exists beyond the material measures!

जो यह लीला हित सो गावे सुने सुनावे ।
प्रेम भक्ति सोई पावे सबके जिय में भावे ॥294॥

*jo yaha līlā hita so gāve sune sunāve,*
*prema bhakti soī pāve sabake jiya mẽ bhāve* (294)

One who sings this divine play,
hears it and tells it in a pleasing way,
will attain loving devotion,
and will be endeared for sure
in the heart of every person!

हीन अश्रद्धा निंदक नास्तिक धर्म बहिर्मुख ।
तिनसों कबहु न कहिये तो नाहिन लहे सुख ॥295॥

*hīna aśraddhā nindaka nāstika dharma bahirmukha,*
*tinasõ kabahu na kahiye kahe to nāhina lahe sukha* (295)

The lowly beings who have no faith,
the critics who always hate,
the heretics who love to scaith,
and the defiers of the devout ways,
Never tell them this loving tale,
for if one does,
no joy is ever gained!

भक्त जनन सो कहो जिनके श्रीभागवत धर्म बल ।
ज्यों यमुना के मीन लीन नित रहत यमुना जल ॥296॥

*bhakta janana so kaho jinake śrībhāgavata dharma bala,*
*jyõ yamunā ke mīna līna nita rahata yamunā jala* (296)

Only those who are strengthened
by splendorous *Bhāgavata*,
and its devotional majesties,
tell this tale to those loving devotees!

Like the loyal fishes of Yamunā,
they are eternally immersed
in her supremely loving waters!

यद्यपि सप्त निधि भेदत यमुना निगम बखाने ।
ते तिहिं धाराहिं धार रमत छूवत न जल आने ॥297॥

*yadyapi sapta nidhi bhedata yamunā nigama bakhāne,*
*te tihĩ dhārāhĩ dhāra ramata chūvata na jala āne* (297)

The Vedas sing the praises
of the divine Yamunā,
she who majestically pierces
the course of the seven seas.
Her streams mingle with the seas,
and in their mighty waves and swells,
yet untouched by this union,
pristine as ever, she dwells!

रसिक जनन के संग रहे हरि लीला गावे ।
परम कांत एकांत परम प्रेम रस सोई पावे ॥298॥

*rasika janana ke saṅga rahe hari līlā gāve,*
*parama kānta ekānta parama rasa soī pāve* (298)

One who resides by the side
of ecstatic loving devotees,
singing the divine plays of Hari
and delighting in his glories,
that person alone attains the supreme Beloved,
and serves him forever in solitude,
attaining the supreme ecstasy.
They regain the eternal restitude!

यह उज्वल रस माला कोटि यत्न कर पोई ।
सावधान होय पहरो जिन तोरो मत कोई ॥299॥

*yaha ujjvala rasa mālā koṭi yatna kara poī,*
*sāvadhāna hoya paharo jina toro mata koī* (299)

This is a garland of unblemished ecstasy,
which I have arduously strung
with great intricacies!
Be mindful when you wear,
so that you never break it,
and cherish it with utmost care!

श्रवण कीर्तन सार सुमिरण को हे पुन ।
ज्ञानसार हरि ध्यान सार श्रुत सार गूंथी गुन ॥300॥

*śravaṇa kīrtana sāra sumiraṇa ko he puna,*
*jñānasāra hari dhyāna sāra śruta sāra gū̃thi guna* (300)

This is the essence of it all,
whether it be listening to his praise,
or singing about his charming games,
even remembering his myriad names!
This quintet the quintessence of all knowledge,
whether found through the Vedic texts,
or gained by mindful meditation on Hari
In this quintet they are interwoven indisputably!

अघ हरनी मन हरनी सुंदर प्रेम विस्तरनी ।
नंददास के कंठ बसो नित मंगल करनी ॥301॥

*agha haranī mana haranī sundara prema vistaranī,*
*Nandadāsa ke kaṇṭha baso nita maṅgala karanī* (301)

O beautiful retelling of love!
O vanquisher of misdeeds!
You are skilful in the art
of stealing every heart!
Rest eternally in Nandadāsa's throat.
O the doer of auspicious deeds,
you are the blessed one indeed!

॥इति पंचाध्यायी भाषा संपूर्णा ॥

|| *iti pañcādhyāyī bhāṣā sampūrṇā* ||

So ends the rendition of the quintet.

# Selected Bibliography

## Primary References:


1. Ghosh, M. (ed.) *Nāṭyaśāstram* (Vol.1&2). Calcutta: Manish Granthālaya, 1967.
2. Gokulanātha, *Caurāsī Vaiṣṇavan Kī Vārtā*. Ed., Gabbad, B. Indore: Vaiṣṇava Mitra Maṇḍal, 2005
3. Gokulanātha, *Do Sau Bāvan Vaiṣṇavan Kī Vārtā* (Vol. 3). Ed., Gabbad, B. Indore: Vaiṣṇava Mitra Maṇḍal, 2005
4. Jīvagosvāmipāda, *Śrī Tattvasandarbha*. Ed. Sastri, H. Mathura: Śrī Gadādharagaurahari Press, 1983
5. Lālūbhaṭṭa, *Prameyaratnārṇava of Śrī Bālakṛṣṇa Bhaṭṭa*. Ed. and transl. Mishra, K., Varanasi: Anand Prakashan, 1971
6. Nandadās, *Rasapracura Rāsapañcādhyāyī Evam Tad Rasāmṛta Madhurabhāva Salilā*. Ed. Daga, K. Nagpur: Manmohan Printing Press, 1980
7. Vallabhācārya, *Bhāgavatārtha*: Vol. 1&2. Ed. Goswami, S.M., Jodhpur: Sri Subodhinī Prakāśana Maṇḍal, 1971
8. Vallabhācārya, *Bhāgavatārtha*. Ed. Goswami, S.M., Kolhapur: Śrī Vallabhavidyāpīṭha-Śrī Viṭṭhaleśaprabhucaraṇāśrma Trust, 1983
9. Vallabhācārya, *Puṣṭividhānam*. Ed. Goswami, S., Gujarat: Śrī Vallabhācārya Trust, 2004
10. Vallabhācārya, *Rāsapañcādhyāyī Śrī Subodhinī*. Ed. and transl. Caturvedī, J., Pt., Varanasi: Chaukhambha Bharati Academy, 2017

11. Vallabhācārya, *Ṣoḍaśagranthāḥ*. Ed. Goswami, S.M., Bombay: Śrī Vallabhācārya Trust, 1980
12. Vallabhācārya, *Subodhinī* (Canto 1&2). Bombay: Gujarati Publication, 1986
13. Vallabhācārya, *Subodhinī* (Canto 10). Ed. Goswami, S.M., Kolhapur: Śrīvallabhavidyāpīṭha-Śrīviṭṭhaleśaprabhucaraṇāśrma Trust, 1993
14. Vallabhācārya, *Tatvārtha-dīpa-nibandhaḥ* (Vol. 1&2). Ed. Goswami, S.M., Kolhapur: Śrīvallabhavidyāpīṭha-Śrīviṭṭhaleśaprabhu caraṇāśrma Trust, 1982

## Secondary References:

15. Agrawal, G.K. *Changing Frontiers of Religion*. India: Agra Book Store, 1983
16. Beck, G.L. "Song: Two *Braj Bhāṣā* Versions of the Rāsa Līlā Pancādhyāyī and Their Musical Performance in Vaisnava Worship." In *The Bhāgavata Purāṇa: Sacred Text and Living Tradition* (pp. 181-201). Eds. Gupta, R.M., Valpey, K.R., New York: Columbia University Press, 2013
17. Bennett, P. "Krishna's own Form: Image Worship in Puṣṭi Mārga." In *Journal of Vaiṣṇava Studies*; 1:4 (pp. 34-109), 1993
18. *Bhavan's Journal*, Vol. 33. Mumbai: Bharatiya Vidya Bhavan, 1986
19. Bryant, E.F. "The Date and Provenance of the Bhāgavata Purāṇa and the Vaikunṭha Perumāl Temple." In *Journal of Vaiṣṇava Studies*; 11:1 (pp. 51-80). Virginia: Deepak Heritage Books, 2002
20. Burchette, P.E. Genealogy of Devotion: Bhakti, Tantra, Yoga and Sufism in North India. New York: Columbia University Press, 2019
21. Chaudhury, R. *Ten Schools of The Vedānta* (Part 1). Calcutta: Rabindra Bharti University, 1973
22. Elkman, S.M. *Jīva Gosvāmin's Tattvasandarbha: A Study on the Philosophical and Sectarian Development of the Gauḍīya Vaiṣṇava Movement*, Delhi: Motilal Banarasidass, 1986
23. Goswami, M. *Nādarasa*. Mumbai: Gīta Saṁgīta Sāgara Trust, 2012
24. Gupta, R.M., Valpey, K.R., *The Bhāgavata Purāṇa: Sacred Text and Living Tradition*. New York: Columbia University Press, 2013
25. Haas, G.C.O. *The Daśarūpa: A Treatise on Hindu Dramaturgy by Dhanaṁjaya*. Delhi: Motilal Banarasidass, 1962

26. Haberman, D.L. *Acting as a Way of Salvation: A Study of Rāgānugā Bhakti Sādhanā*. New York: Oxford University Press, 2001
27. Hume, R. *The Thirteen Principal Upanishads: Translated from the Sanskrit with an Outline of the Philosophy of the Upanishads and an Annotated Bibliography*. England: Oxford University Press, 1921
28. Karṇapūra, *Ānanda Vṛndāvana Campū*, The University of Michigan Press, 1999.
29. McIntosh, S. *Hidden Faces of Ancient Indian Song*. Burlington: Ashgate Publishing, 2005
30. Meyer-Dinkgräfe, D. *Approaches to Acting: Past and Present*. London: Continuum, 2005
31. Meyer-Dinkgräfe, D. (ed.) *Consciousness, Literature, Theatre, and the Arts 2011*. Newcastle upon Tyne: Cambridge Scholars Publishing 2012
32. Nicholson, A.J. *Unifying Hinduism: Philosophy and Identity in Indian Intellectual History*. New York: Columbia University Press, 2013
33. Radhakrishnan, S. *The Principal Upaniṣads*. Noida: HarperCollins Publishers, 2014
34. Ranade, A.D. *Music Contexts: A Concise Dictionary of Hindustani Music*. New Delhi: Promilla & CO. Publishers, 2006
35. Redington, J.D. *The Grace of Lord Krishna: The Sixteen Verse-Treatises (Ṣoḍaśagranthāḥ) of Vallabhacharya*. Delhi: Sri Satguru Publications, 2000
36. Rukumani, T.S. *A Critical Study of the Bhāgavata Purāṇa*. Varanasi: Chaukhamba Sanskrit Series, 1970
37. Sanyal, R., Widdess, R. *Dhrupad: Tradition and Performance in Indian Music* (Vol.1). Ashgate, 2004
38. Schweig, G.M. *Dance of Divine Love*. Princeton: Princeton University Press, 2005
39. Shankar, R. *Raga Mala: The Autobiography of Ravi Shankar*. Ed. Harrison, G. New York: Welcome Rain Publishers, 1999
40. Sāstrī, S.S. *Saṁgītaratnākara* (Vol. II). Chennai: The Adyar Library and Research Centre, 1959.
41. Shastri, A.D. *Puruṣottamjī: A Study*. Surat: Chunilal Gandhi Vidyabhava, 1966
42. Smith, F. "Nirodha And The Nirodhalakṣaṇa Of Vallabhācārya." In *Journal of Indian Philosophy*; 26 (pp. 489-551), 1998.

43. Smith, F. "Predestination and Hierarchy." In *Journal of Indian Philosophy*; 39 (pp. 173-227), 2011
44. Te Nijenhuis, E. *Dattilam: A Compedium of Ancient Indian Music.* Leiden: E.J. Brill, 1970
45. Theodor, I. "The Pariṇāma Aesthetics as Underlying the Bhāgavata Purāṇa." In *Asian Philosophy: And International Journal of the Philosophical Traditions of the East*; 17:2 (pp. 109-12). Routledge, 2007
46. Thielemann, S. *The Music of South Asia.* The University of Michigan Press, 1999
47. Timm, J.R. "Prolegomenon to Vallabha's Theology of Revelation." In *Philosophy of East and West*; 38:2 (pp. 107-126). University of Hawai'i Press, 1988
48. Wade, B.C. *Imaging Sound: An Ethnomusicological Study of Music, Art, and Culture in Mughal India.* Chicago: University of Chicago Press, 1998
49. Wulff, D.M. "Drama as a Mode of Religious Realization – The Vidagdhamādhava of Rūpa Gosvāmī." In AAR Academy Series; 43. CA: Scholars Press, 1984

# Index


Abhinavagupta, 13–14
aesthetics
  concepts, 12
  definitions, 16
  expressions, 13
*Ain-I-Akbari* of Abu Fazl, *Dhrupad in*, 25
Akbar, Mughal emperor, 36
*ālāpa*, 22
*ālāpacārī*, 30
*anavatāra-kāla and avatāra-kāla*, 33, 38
Anuśayana, 16–17
*āśraya*, 15–16
*aṣṭa-chāpas*, 19, 21, 26, 32–33
Aurangzeb, 28
*avyāvṛttaḥ*, 6

Beck, Guy L., 22, 25
beginning of the creation (sargaparamparayā-avicchedana), 8
belongingness to Kṛṣṇa (*kṛṣṇa-tavāsmi*), 38
*Bhagavadgītā*, 5
*Bhagavān*, 5
  Kṛṣṇa as, 7
*Bhāgavata-bhakti* traditions, 23–24
*Bhāgavata Purāṇa*, 3–5
  āśraya, 15
  bhakti movements, 13
  devotion to Kṛṣṇa, 15
  dramatic nature, 14
  Kṛṣṇa devotional motifs, 5–6
  nirodha, 15–16
  practice of *sevā, 31*
  relevance of *dhrupad, 25*
  thematic categorization, 15
  theo-aesthetics, 11–13
bhakti, 25–26, 31, 39
  as bhajanānanda (bliss of worshipping), 17
  bhakti-rasa, 14, 18
  Kṛṣṇa-*bhakti,* Braja tradition, 21
  regional forms and styles, 4
*bhakti*-saints, 26
*basanta, 30*
*bhāva and rasa*, 38
  relation between, 13–14
  Sanskritic aesthetic theory, 13
*bhāva-prakāṣa*, 35
Bhedavāda (Doctrine of Difference) of Madhva, 5
Bhoja, 13–14

Birbal, 36
*Brahman* (formless Absolute), 5–8, 10, 12, 14, 18
  āśraya. notion of, 16
  brahmāṃśa, part of Brahman, 7
  creation as a cosmic play of, 10
  in the form of Kṛṣṇ, 18
  manifestation of, 7
  sat and cit aspects, 8
*brahmānanda* (bliss of attaining oneness with the impersonal Brahman). 17
*Brahmasūtras*, 4–5, 18
Braja
  folk culture of, 26–27
  Mathura-gharānā, 28
  region, 25
*Braja-bhāṣa*, 32
Bṛhadāraṇyaka Upaniṣad, 14
*Bṛhaddeśi, 23*

Caitanya tradition, 33
*Chanda*, 22
creation, 6, 8, 10, 16, 21, 30
cycle of births and deaths, 8

daily worship, 31–32, 37
*Dattilam*, 22
deity, 7, 9, 14–15, 21
delightful play (ramaṇa), 14
*deśi* music, 48 varieties, 23
devotees, 6–7, 9–11, 14–18, 28, 31–33, 35. *See also* gopikās
devotion, 18, 28, 31–33, 38–41, 46
  in Bhāgavata, 11–12
  categories, 8
  gopikās, 9–10
  in Nandadāsa's devotional poetry, 6
  theo-aesthetics of Kṛṣṇa worship, 11
  Vallabha tradition. 6, 9–10, 15
devotional-aesthetic (bhakti-rasa), 14
devotional worship, 18
  processes, 13
*dhamār* and the *cautāla* are common musical meters, 29
Dhondhī, 28
*dhrupad-dhamār* style, 29–30
*Dhruvapada/dhrupad,* 24
Dhrupad era, 26, 30
  *abhogī*.29
  *antarā*, 29
  *cauguna*, 29
  *cautāla*, 29
  *core themes*, 25
  *dhamār*, 29
  *dhrupad*, 22, 24–25, 30
  *duguna*, 29
  *jhapatāla*, 29
  *sañcārī*, 29
  *sthāyī*, 29
  structured songs, 24–25
divine bliss (ānandasya harerlīlā), 7
divine grace or *puṣṭi-puruśottama*. 6, 9–10, 39–40
divine play (ramaṇa), 18
divine will. 7
dramaturgy, 11, 45
*Dvaita*, 18

ecstasy, 24
Ecstatic Dance (Verses 223–286), 127–150
eight poet-devotees. *See aṣṭa-chāpas*
*ekāgraha* (one-pointed devotion), 8
elongated vowels (*stobhas*), 22
emotions, 7, 10, 13, 24, 32, 38

forms of (sarva-bhāvena), 7
everlasting divine play (*nitya-līlā*), 40
fear (*bhaya*), 38

*Gandharva, 22*
Gauḍiya Vaiṣṇava tradition, 24
Gokulotsavajī Mahārāja. Pt, 28, 30
gopikās, 7, 9–10, 16–18
archetype of devotion, 33, 36–39
as *antaḥ-gṛha-gataḥ*, 18
eight primary gopikās (aṣṭa-sakhis), 33, 36
erotic desire (jārabhāva) of, 18
music knowledge, 24–26, 31
passionate love, 32
*śrutis* as, 18
grace, 3, 6, 8–10, 33
grace-filled selves (*puṣṭi-jīvas*), 8
gṛhe-sthitvā, 6

Haridās, 28
Harirām Vyās, 26
*Braja-bhāṣā* rendition, 34
Harirāya, 35–36
*Havelī Saṅgīta*. 19, 21, 23, 25–26
*ālāpacārī* or *ālāpa*, 30
calatī, 29
liturgical and exegetical use, 31–34
parental love of Yaśodā, 28
passionate love of the *gopikās*, 28
prabandha, 30
roles of both Yaśodā and the *gopikās*, 31
structure, 27–31
*ṭappā*, 30
*ṭhumrī*, 30
Hindustani Classical. *See Dhrupad*
Hindu traditions, 31–34
worship and liturgy, 21
humble servitude (*dāsa-bhāva*). 39

inappropriate nature (*svabhāva*), 8
Indian devotional music. *See also* Dhrupad era; *prabandha* music
classical from (north and south), 23
classical, 22, 137–38
concept of rāga (melodic mode), 23
deśi music (regional), 23
devotional, 21–23
*gandharva- saṅgīta*, 22
*mārgi* music (classical), 23
regional, 27, 30
role in worship, 21
*Sāmaveda/sāma-gāna*, 22
*saragama* (notations), or sol-fa), 23
secular, 22–23
Vaiṣṇava devotional singing, 24
individual egoism (*ahaṃkāra*), 10
inexcusable action (karma), 8

*Janamāṣṭamī* (the birth of Kṛṣṇa), 32
jewels, 26, 49
*jhānjha, 25*
jīvas, 8

Kaṭha Upaniṣad, 9
Kavi Karṇapūra, *Ānanda Vṛndāvana,* 24
*Kevalādvaita* (Absolute Monism) of Śaṃkara, 5
*khayāl* singing. 29–30
*kīrtana-bhakti, 25*
knowledge of one's own self (*svarūpa-jñāna*), 7
knowledge, 5, 7, 14–15, 22, 24, 33

*Kṛṣṇa-bhakti* and *Kṛṣṇa-līlā*
*Dhrupad*, 26–27
Kṛṣṇa, the supreme deity
as *brahmānanda*, 18
chosen (*varaṇa*), 8
cognitive-spiritual awareness, 7
dweller of Braja" (*brajavāsī*), 31
as Lord of Vraja, 7
paradoxical qualities, 6
as the supreme Self, 18
Kṛṣṇa's Solace to the Gopikās (Verses 196–222), 117–126

līlātmika-dvaita, 14
love for God (*sneha*), 6

*mādhurya-bhāva* (love of the gopikās),7
*māhātmya*, 6
*malhāra, 30*
manifestation, 7–8, 10, 14, 18
Man Singh Tomar of Gwalior, 25–26
*Braja-bhāṣā, 25*
*apabhraṁśa*) of Prākṛta,26
*viṣṇupadas* (praise of Lord Viṣṇu), 26
*dhrupads*, 26–27
*dhamār/horī* (Kṛṣṇa celebrating the festival of Holi). 26
*maryādā-bhakti* or duty-bound devotion, 39
*maryādā-jīvas* as godly, 8
*maryādā-puruśottama* or Lord Rāma, 39
Mātaṅga, 23
material possessions (*mamatā*), 38
mood, 14–15, 30, 32, 39, 72
and rasa, 138
tranquillity (*śānta-rasa*), 39
Motilal Banarasidass, 13, 16
Mukundarāyajī Mahārāja, Pt, 28–29
revival of the original *dhrupad* compositions, 29
*Nādarasa, 29*
*Muṇḍaka Upaniṣad*, 21
musical tradition, 25, 27–28

*nāda (sound), 21*
Nandadāsa, 17, 19, 40
abstruse and exotic nature of compositions, 40
aṣṭa-chāpa, 3, 19
Candrarekhā, divine form of, 36
devotional worship of Rāma (Rāmānandī), 36
Ecstatic Dance (Verses 223–286), 127–150
inception of nirodha. 37–38
journey to Gokul, 36–37
Kṛṣṇa's Solace to the Gopikās (Verses 196–222), 117–126
Pangs of Separation (Verses 134–180), 93–109
poetic rendition, 19
rāsa dance,34
Rāsalīlā, beginning of (Verses 55–133), 65–92)
rāsapañcādhyāyī, 21, 30, 40
Song of the Gopikās (Verses 181–195), 111–116
41 songs on Yamunā (iktālis-pada), 37
Śuka-Stuti (Verses 1–21), 45–51
241st disciple of Viṭṭhalanātha, 36
Vṛndāvana-Varṇana (Verses 22–54), 53–63

Nārada, 22
Nāṭyaśāstra, 14, 22–24
  aesthetic theory, 13
*Nimbārka* sect, 26
*nirguṇa Brahman*, 5
*nirguṇa-bhakti* for Kṛṣṇa. 37
nirodha. 15–17
non-duality (advaita), 7
  awareness of, 15
  and playful duality, 15

object of devotion (*niṣṭhā*), 39
own self (*ahantā*), 38

*pada* (word), 22
*pañcādhyāyī*, 17
  arrival of the gopikās, 17
*pañca-Vedānta-sampradāya*. 5
Pangs of Separation (Verses 134–180), 93–109
passion, 7, 14, 17, 28–29, 37, 39
period of time (kāla), 8
*Phala-Śruti*: Significance of the Mahārāsa (287–301), 151–157
physical body (*tana*), 6
play of Kṛṣṇa (*nitya-līlā*), 5
playacting (*līlā*), 17
playful duality (*līlātmaka-dvaita*), 7, 14
power, 10, 16–17
*prabandha* music
  *dhruva songs*, 23–24
  *sālaga-sūḍa*, 23
  *śuddha-sūḍa*, 23–24
*pramāṇa-catuṣṭaya* (four-fold means of knowledge). 5
*prapañcavismṛti*, 17
*pravāhī-jīvas as āsurī*, 8
Purāṇic scriptures, 4
"Pure Non-dualism" (Śuddhādvaita), 14
passionate form of bhakti (madhurya-pradhānabhakti), 15
*Puruṣottama*, 8–10
puṣṭi, definition, 8–9
*Puṣṭimārga*, 3–6, 19, 21, 26–33, 37–38, 41
  Holi celebration, 26
  musical legacy, 21
*Puṣṭipravāhamaryādabheda*, 8

Rādhā's Kṛṣṇa worship, 40
Raṇchoḍa, Lord, 36
*Rasa*, eight types of, 13
*Rāsalīlā*, beginning of Verses 55–133), 65–92)
*rāsa-līlā*, Kṛṣṇa's dance of divine love, 3, 32
*rāsapañcādhyāyī*, 3, 13–19, 23
  of the Bhāgavata, 10
Raskhān, 26, 28
rati (passionate love), 14
Ravi Shankar, Pt, *Dhrupad singing,* 25
resentment (*dveṣa*), 38
*Ṛgveda, 22*
rule-bound selves (maryādā-jīvas), 8
Rūpa Gosvāmī. *rāgānugā-bhakti,* 31

*śabda-pradhāna-gāyakī*, 29
sages, 22–23, 50
salvation, 14, 17, 26
*Samāja Gāyana,* 25–26, 30
*samarpaṇa*, 6
*saṃnyāsa*, 13
*saṃsāra*, 19
Sanat, 152,

Sanandana, 152
San*ātana, 152*
Sanatkum*āra*, 152
Classical aesthetic theory of India,
 *bhāva* and *rasa*. 13
Śārṅgāradeva
 Saṅgīta Ratnākara, 23
 77 varieties, 23
*sarvadā, 7*
*Śāstrārtha, 6, 12*
 distinguishing feature, 6
*sthāyībhāva, 13*
 meaning, 13
 *śṛṅgāra-rasa* (mood of passion), 14
scriptures, 4–5, 18, 33
service of Kṛṣṇa, 38
*sevā,* Vallabha's concept, 6–7
*sevya-svarūpa* (Kṛṣṇa-for-worship), 31
*sevya-svarūpa, 6*
Shyam Manohar Goswami, 30
Song of the Gopikās (Verses 181–195),
 111–116
soteriological effect, 10, 17,19
Śrīnāthajī temple (mount Govardhana), 21, 28
*śṛṅgāra-rasa, 14*
*Śrutis, 33*
*śrutis, gopikās as, 18*
*śuddha* (undiluted devotion), 8, 10
*Śuddhādvaita* (Pure Non-dualism) of
 Vallabha. 5–6, 9, 14
*śuddha-puṣṭi-bhakti,* 10
*śudhha-prema,* 38
Sufism, 4
Śuka-Stuti (Verses 1–21), 45–51
supreme Lord, 8, 10–11, 16, 18, 32–33,
 39, 41
 definition, 10
supreme self (brahmānanda). 19
supreme Self, 7, 14, 18–19, 21
*Svābhāvikadvaitādvaita*
 (Natural Dualism-Non-dualism) of
 Nimbārka, 5
Svāmī Haridās, 26
*svara* (tone), 22

*Taittirīya Upaniṣad,* 16
*tāla* (beat), 22
*tāla, 25*
Tānsen, 26, 28
 father of Hindustani Classical
 music, 26
 *nava-ratanas, 26*
 *Havelī Saṅgīta* compositions, 26
Tattvasandarbha, 15
Tulasīdās, Saint, 36, 38
 and Lord Rāma, 39

unconditional love, 31
*Upaniṣads,* 5, 13

Vaiṣṇava Mitra, 33, 35–37, 39–40
Vaiṣṇava Worship, 22, 25, 34
*Vārtā* literature, 32–33
*vātsalya-bhāva (*love of Yaśodā), 7
Vallabha tradition, 3–4
 *Bhāgavata-Bhakti,* 12
 *Bhāva,* definition, 14
 concept of *sevā,* 6
 conceptualisation of
 *puṣṭi-bhakti,* 10
 definition of *āśraya,* 16
 *devotion,* 6, 9–10, 15
 devotional music tradition, 25
 on ideal devotee, 7
 puṣṭi, definition, 8
 sixteen treatises, 8
 three-fold hierarchization, 8

on Lord's grace (*prameya-bala*), 33
vārtā literature or Vārtājī
stories of 84 disciples of Vallabha, 35
stories of 252 disciples of Viṭṭhalanātha, 35
Gokulanātha, author of, 34
Recurring theme, 41
Vedānta schools, 4–5, 10–12
epistemological structure, 4–5
Vedic age
discipline. 39
music in, 21
text, 4, 33, 156
*Viśiṣṭādvaita* (Qualified Monism) of Rāmānuja, 5
Viṭṭhalanātha, 28, 40
*bhoga-rāga-śṛṅgāra*. 28
Vallabha's son, 32
Vraja, 6
*Vṛndāvana* or *Goloka*, 26
Vṛndāvana-Varṇana (Verses 22–54), 53–63

worldly selves (*pravāhī-jīvas*), 8
worldly-selves, 8
worship, 6, 11, 21, 25, 27–28, 31–32
devotional, 13, 18, 27, 36
meditative, 18

yamunā, 37, 40
Yaśodā', Parental love, 32
*yaśodotsangalālitya, 6*
yogic meditation (*dhyāna-dhāraṇa*), 39

MANDALA
An Imprint of MandalaEarth
PO Box 3088
San Rafael, CA 94912
www.MandalaEarth.com

Find us on Facebook: www.facebook.com/MandalaEarth
Follow us on Twitter: @MandalaEarth

–

Publisher Raoul Goff
Associate Publisher Phillip Jones
Editorial Director Katie Killebrew
VP Creative Chrissy Kwasnik
Art Director Ashley Quackenbush
VP Manufacturing Alix Nicholaeff
Sr Production Manager Joshua Smith
Sr Production Manager, Subsidiary Rights Lina s Palma-Temena


Layout design by Eight Eyes Design



ISBN: 978-1-64722-919-1

Manufactured in India by Insight Editions
10 9 8 7 6 5 4 3 2 1

ROOTS of PEACE REPLANTED PAPER

Insight Editions, in association with Roots of Peace, will plant two trees for each tree used in the manufacturing of this book. Roots of Peace is an internationally renowned humanitarian organization dedicated to eradicating land mines worldwide and converting war-torn lands into productive farms and wildlife habitats. Roots of Peace will plant two million fruit and nut trees in Afghanistan and provide farmers there with the skills and support necessary for sustainable land use.